FOREWORD BY JAMES GOLL

AN ARMY ARISING
to
SHIFT THE NATIONS

CHERYL L. LINDLEY

"An Army Arising to Shift the Nations"
by Cheryl L. Lindley
Published by
ARC Global (Apostolic Restore Community)
PO Box 4393
Helensvale B.C. QLD 4212
Australia

This book or parts thereof may not be reproduced in any form, stored in a retrieval system, or transmitted in any form by any means – electronic, mechanical, photocopy, recording or otherwise – without prior written permission of the publisher, except as provided by Australian copyright law.

All New Testament scripture, including the Books of Psalms and Proverbs are quotations from The Passion Translation of the Bible unless otherwise stated.

All Old Testament scripture excluding the Books of Psalms and Proverbs are quotations from the New Living Version 2011 of the Bible unless otherwise specified.

Scriptures marked NLT are taken from the HOLY BIBLE, New Living Translation, Copyright © 2015 by Tyndale House. Used by permission of Tyndale House. All rights reserved.

Scriptures taken from the HOLY BIBLE, The Passion Translation (TPT) Copyright © 2017

Copyright © 2021 Cheryl Lindley (Revised Edition)
Cover design by Rachel Lindley
ISBN: 978-0-9942402-8-6
Printed in Australia

Dedication

An Army Arising to Shift the Nations is dedicated to my Lord: The Father, Son and Holy Spirit, in whom I live and move and have my being. It is my great privilege, joy and delight to serve His Kingdom.

This book is also dedicated to my wonderful husband Bruce, the best cheerleader anyone could ask for. It is also for my dear children, their spouses and my grandchildren, whom I pray will find their encouragement and inspiration in this book.

It is also dedicated, to the most spectacular of parents, Noel and Doreen Woodford, who have unrelentingly loved me.

And to the bravest, kindest, and most faithful Firehouse team anyone could wish to serve alongside! To everyone who has fought alongside me over the years through the many battles, I salute you. You have been a constant source of strength and encouragement as God has led us across nations to bring Jesus the glory due His name.

Acknowledgements

I would like to thank all who helped complete this book.

The first thank you must go to our wonderful friend James Goll, who so kindly volunteered to write the foreword to this book.

Heartfelt thanks also to our dear friend Patricia King. Thank you for your years of encouragement.

Thank you also to Jenny Haggar, a General of Faith in our nation who has been a role model to aspire to.

A huge thank you also to Adrian Beale, a legendary prophetic teacher and friend who keeps me theologically sound.

Thank you to Paul & Pamela Segneri for their amazing editing skills and all their help in getting this book finished.

Big hugs of thanks to my talented daughter, Rachel, who did such a wonderful job with the cover design and also contributed to the editing.

Lastly, a very special thank you to my husband Bruce, for his constant love, encouragement and facilitation in seeing this project completed.

Endorsements

Jesus gave the church authority in the earth to establish His Kingdom and to make disciples of nations. Cheryl Lindley has committed herself to this mandate for many years. She has faithfully and effectively taught, led, and mobilized intercessors with vision and skill for impacting nations. Her book, *An Army Arising to Shift the Nations,* is one that every believer should read in the midst of a season when the world is full of crisis, confusion, darkness, and turmoil. This is the hour for the Body to arise unto this very mandate. I endorse both Cheryl Lindley and this wonderful book.

PATRICIA KING
AUTHOR, MINISTER, TELEVISION HOST

This insightful book has been written by an internationally recognised warrior who has had many experiences fighting on the front lines. In the thrust of battle she has gained a wealth of revelation and prophetic insight that she now shares for the equipping of others.

Her clear biblical teaching, practical outlines and ground breaking testimonies are a valuable tool not only for intercessors but for all who are called to be part of God's rising army to shift nations; including apostles, prophets, evangelists, pastors and teachers. I highly recommend this book for the advancement of the Kingdom.

Jenny Hagger AM
Founder and Director Australian House of
Prayer For All Nations

As you read Cheryl Lindley's new book you will feel the call to open your wings afresh and take up your position amidst an awakening army of prophetic warriors to see the nations changed and the kingdom established throughout the earth.

Adrian Beale
THEDIVINITYCODE.ORG

Contents

Foreword by James G. Goll 11

Introduction 15

Part One: An Army Arising 23

Chapter 1: Raise Up an Army 25

Chapter 2: Revelations to Advance the Kingdom of Heaven in the Nations 41

Chapter 3: More Revelations to Advance the Kingdom of Heaven in the Nations 55

Chapter 4: How Joshua Enforced a New Era 69

Chapter 5: God's Authority in Bringing in a New Era 85

Chapter 6: A New Army for a New Era 93

Chapter 7: Specialist Forces in the Kingdom Army 107

Chapter 8: The Lifestyle and Personal Profile of the Watchman 139

Part Two: Shift the Nations 161

Chapter 9: God's Strategy for the Nations 163

Chapter 10: Authority to Shift Nations 181

Chapter 11: Shifting Nations 205

Chapter 12: Prayer Strikes 231

Chapter 13: Commissioned into a Movement 257

Endnotes 267

Appendix

Appendix:1: Charlie Shamp's full prophetic word. 277

Appendix 2: Decrees that Shift Nations. 281

Foreword

BY JAMES GOLL

The scriptures have a lot to say about 3's. A three-cord strand will not be quickly torn apart. Where two or three are brought together, there Jesus is in their midst. God in three Persons: Father, Son and Holy Spirit… and God has made us in the image of God: Spirit, Soul and Body.

As a leader and an author, I keep my eyes open for the combination of three key components in the lives of others; in what they live, in what they teach and in what they write. What could these three significant ingredients be?

I am constantly on the search for those who are grounded in the Word of God, live the Word of God and carry a distinct cutting edge of the Word of God in their lives. Oh, that is a combination of another three, if you did not notice. Yes, it takes character to carry the gift of God long term. In my lifetime, I have seen too many fast-rising 'shooting stars' in the body of Christ who act more like the world than they do the Word. They often rise quickly with great notoriety, before the eyes of many, with a flare and flame, to only become 'falling stars' and another casualty and disappointment. But it need not be that way.

That is why, when I was approached to compose the Foreword for this balanced and yet edgy book by Cheryl Lindley, I gave an immediate 'YES!' This dear woman of God is Prayer personified. There are some who pray prayers. There are some who teach others how to pray. Then there are some who are PRAYER itself. There are some who believe truth. There are some who teach others truth. Then there are some who are TRUTH itself.

Then there is another component that is contained within these pages. It is the reality of progressive revelation. Consider the following examples that my friend of years, Cheryl Lindley, brings forth. There is a 'New Army for a New Era!' In fact, she is bold enough to state, there are 'Special Forces in this New Army of God' such as a 'Company of Watchman!' Then Cheryl has the audacity to lift the vision higher beyond a personal perspective into a global strategy on how to shift entire nations through prayers that strike the mark!

Now, let me take it further. Previously, I have been one of the few who have written on the subject on 'The Lifestyle of a Prophet' and 'The Lifestyle of a Watchman.' But not any longer! This prophetic prayer manual you hold in your hand also addresses the 'Lifestyle and Personal Profile of the Watchman'. By the way, I just stood to my feet and gave a big shout-out!

Now, it's your turn! Are you hungry for more? Do you want your life to make a difference? Do you believe that two and three brought together in agreement in Christ Jesus can make history? Then read and apply! Yes, then read and apply the principles and truths found in these strategic pages.

Blessings to All!

James W. Goll
Founder of God Encounters Ministries
GOLL Ideation LLC

Introduction

I have been completing this book in 2020 as the CoVid-19 pandemic continues to buffet the nations. It seems not one nation or people group has been exempt from the need to make changes to accommodate the new circumstance that the world finds itself in. CoVid-19, Black Lives Matter, riots across nations and economic recession have caused the nations to reel.

As always, God, our heavenly Father and the Father of the Nations, has an answer! We are never without hope in this world!

Can you hear it? It is the sound of an army, emerging out of their hiding places, to stand tall and strong in this New Era of God's power released in the earth. Day after day, they are joined with new recruits! The sound is getting louder. It is the rising of the army of God!

The people of God have the answer the world is waiting for! The earth has been waiting; groaning to see the sons and daughters of God rise and shine! It is time for the wait to be over and that the sons and daughters of God be revealed as overcomers who are calling the people and nations into freedom! (Romans 8:19-21)

It's time! It is time to enforce Jesus' victory in every sector of society throughout the nations. Amidst the turmoil, there is an awakening, there is a rising, there is the sound of an army coming forth, ringing bells of victory out across the land. It is the imminent release of Jesus' sure victory over all the power of the enemy currently assaulting the nations.

The kingdom of darkness is attempting to use the calamities erupting across the nations to take more and more ground. Fear, unbelief, chaos, poverty, division, and death have risen up in nations in an attempt to take dominion in the earth in greater measure.

This should not be! Jesus, through His death and resurrection, has overcome all the power of the enemy. Now the only right and just outcome for the lives of every man and woman on earth is to overcome the power of the enemy and receive their inheritance of righteousness, peace and joy.

Step Up. Don't back down. The Lord has need of you. It is time for war!

It is time for every son and daughter of God to enlist in the army of God to which we are called. It is an Army that has the authority of Christ to overcome all the power of the enemy to win the lost and disciple nations!

This army of God is no longer intimidated by the hand of the enemy. They are rising to 'rule in the midst of their enemies' and call the nations back to the Lordship of Christ.

This new era is demanding that the overcomers rise into a whole new dimension of overcoming power to rescue the nations.

God is fashioning an army equal to the battle ahead. Life is changing and re-arranging. By necessity, a re-ordering and re-alignment has come into the lives of His people, so that His Kingdom is prepared to powerfully advance across the nations.

There is a sound of a movement rising. A movement releasing a sound of victory! It is the sound of an army rising to declare, 'Prepare the way of the Lord! Make way for the King!'

Proclaim, 'His Kingdom has come to the nations and there is a glorious harvest and home-coming for the people'.

A Prophetic Picture

Toward the end of 2019, before we had heard of CoVid-19, although it may possibly had already begun, I saw a picture in the Spirit:

> *I caught a quick glimpse of my daughter Rachel and me in a boat about seven metres long. It was a people-mover, so it had quite a few people on board, although it wasn't full. We were all wearing life jackets. The captain was facing forward, steering the 'ship.'*
>
> *As we bobbled sideways over a wave, I gazed backward to see the next wave coming. It was a gigantic wave, a wall of water, about thirty metres high, just cresting. It took*

my breath away and my heart sank. I reached over to my daughter as if to brace her for what was coming.

I understood that Rachel, her name meaning lamb, represented the body of Christ. The lifejackets meant that we had the life of Christ and His protection with us. I saw that Jesus was the captain of the vessel and that the huge wave was a wave of turmoil across the sea of humanity.

Initially, this picture overwhelmed me. I could not see that there was any way out. Yet as I meditated on this picture, I was encouraged that Jesus was the Captain at the helm. I saw that He was able to take the boat and ride the wave like a surfboard across the face of the wave, catch it as it barrelled over and deliver those on the boat into their destiny with a powerful force and great momentum.

We know now that the world is in the midst of a violent and tumultuous surge at the hand of the CoVid pandemic and the resultant dilemmas associated to it. It may seem overwhelming and disturbing to realise the situation we are in. However, I believe that as we position ourselves in the Father's protection and trust Jesus in the midst of the crisis, Jesus has a way out for us.

It may be a little alarming to go through the situations we will find ourselves in. It may be a little overwhelming to see the speed at which we find ourselves catapulted along in order to be freed from the situation. However, if we will allow the Lord to take the helm, He will manoeuvre us out of the danger and use it to catapult us, His people and nations, into destiny.

You can trust the captain. Don't jump ship relying on your own strength. Even with a life jacket you will not make it. 'Hang on' tightly entwined with Him, for He is using powerful forces in this time to position His people for future and destiny.

It may look scary; it may take your breath away, however Jesus is able to navigate the way for you. In fact, trusting Him and staying in the vessel is our only chance. He is working 'all' things together for the good of those who love Him and are called according to His purposes!

In fact, we can embrace the challenge, enjoy the heights and thrill at the speed at which our destiny and the destiny of the nations is being outworked in the earth.

God is determined to keep His covenant promise to bring His people and the nations into their inheritance. He is faithful to keep covenant with all those individuals, families, people groups and nations who have called Him their God.

Many nations of the earth over the last 2000 years have declared that their nations would live under the Judaeo-Christian premise and laws because of the Lordship of Jesus in the earth. These nations have flourished and prospered until, like Israel of old, they have forsaken the laws and standards of God. We see, as in history past, a slow eroding of righteousness in the nations, with the resultant loss of peace, stability and freedom for their people.

The battle for the nations and the people of God within these nations who uphold the righteous cause of Christ continues to rage. This battle will continue to rage until the kingdoms of this world are subdued by the Kingdom of our Lord. We, the people of God, are at war in ever-increasing measure, and to finally win this war, the church must embrace this mindset and rise as the army that we are called to be.

I heard the Lord say:

My hand is outstretched to orchestrate a New Era of My Kingdom on the earth.

Now is the time, the kairos time of my favour, a time when My divine will has gone before My people to activate them into My plans and purposes.

The preparations have been completed and now it is time for the flourishing of My bride across the earth.

There will be a new way in this new day. In this year of 2020, I have called you to see with 2020 vision: look intently, call out for insight, ask for wisdom to navigate the new way necessary for this new day. I have a great and mighty army arising in the earth. Cry out as Solomon for wisdom and understanding on how to emerge as this 'new-look' army of My precious people across the earth.

The old is now obsolete and fading away. Do not look back, do not long for the old or you will find a way to go back! As in the quote, 'If you always do what you always did, you'll always get what you always got!'

Look up! Expect the new and different. Facilitate the new in the new day.

Now is the time to embrace the new ways for these new days!'

In this book I want to infuse you with HOPE! I want to encourage us all as believers to rise and be the champions, the warriors of Light in this world that God has called us to be. I want to infuse you with courage to rise up and take your inheritance.

This book is also written to give understanding to the necessity of a 'new-look' Army of God for this New Era. God is fashioning an army equal to the battle ahead. Life is changing and re-arranging in this new CoVid world. God is using this time. He is bringing a divine re-ordering into the lives of His people, so that His Kingdom is prepared to powerfully advance across the nations.

It is time for every son and daughter of God to enlist in the army of God to which we are called. It is an Army that has the authority of Christ to overcome all the power of the enemy to win the lost and disciple nations!

There is a sound of a movement rising. A movement releasing a sound of victory! It is the sound of an army rising to declare,

'Prepare the way of the Lord; Make way for the King!'

Proclaim, 'His Kingdom has come to the nations and there is a glorious harvest and home-coming for the peoples!

There is a call for the whole body of Christ, the army of God, to rise into the fullness of their authority in this escalating battle between light and darkness! God is activating His warriors in the heavens and on the earth. It is time for the church of Jesus Christ to take up their authority and rule in the midst of their enemies, to release light in the darkness, command great shifts and reap a great harvest in the nations.

Part One

An Army Arising

CHAPTER 1

Raise Up an Army

Rise and Shine!

I came so that they would have life, and have it abundantly. — John 10:10 (NASB)

Beloved ones, it is God's great desire that the world He made, and the people all across the globe, whom He loves, experience abundant life! This is the dream on God's heart, and He has spent thousands of years bringing this dream to reality. It is closer today than ever before.

Dear ones, He is calling us in this New Era to 'Rise and Shine,' for now is His 'appointed time' in the earth to bring the nations to life and hope and the peoples to know the Truth. This Truth that can only be discovered through a people who will rise as an army and shine the Light of the gospel across the nations of the globe.

As the Lord of Hosts rises with His army, He is offering us the privilege of 'fighting' with the Host of Heaven's armies to win people, people groups and nations into the Kingdom of God. It is time for war! It is time for the nations to be shifted back under the government of God! God can 'shift' the nations through you!

There is a call and empowering of the body of Christ right now to 'Rise' like Jesus and the early church in the power of the Holy Spirit.

It takes courage, boldness, confidence, strength and the fierceness of the Lion of Judah within to rise regardless of what is standing against us in the quest to advance the Kingdom.

It also takes the meekness of the Lamb to 'Shine' in a surrendered life full of compassion before others and be the light of healing, restoration, and the miraculous power of Christ to them. Like Jesus the Lamb, it will mean laying down our lives in one way or another. It will also take great wisdom to know when to rise in the power of the Lion and when to surrender as the Lamb.

The army called to rise in the earth is like Nehemiah's army. It is an army that knows that it is necessary to be adept with both hands. It is an army that can fight and build at the same time.

Nehemiah 4:16-17

'The leaders stationed themselves behind the people of Judah who were building the wall. The labourers carried on their work with one hand supporting their load and one hand holding a weapon. All the builders had a sword belted to their side'.

It is an army that has heard the call of Jeremiah:

Jeremiah 1:9-10

'Look, I have put my words in your mouth!
Today I appoint you to stand up against nations and kingdoms.
Some you must uproot and tear down, destroy and overthrow.
Others you must build up and plant'.

Unlike the Old Testament warriors, we fight to secure what Jesus has already won. The enemy only has authority where there has been agreement with his unrighteous dictates down the generations and in the present. This has meant the usurping of Christ's authority, and it has allowed his hordes to wreak havoc in the earth.

We are called to be like Jesus and to rise and release the power, boldness and authority of the Lion of Judah against the enemies of the Kingdom of God. We are also called to shine the light of life, love and the laid-down nature of the Lamb of God to display His goodness to advance the Kingdom.

It takes an overcoming spirit to do both, and the Lord is calling forth His army in such a manner.

You Are His Champion!

Hebrews 8 declares that God has given His people a new heart and a new mind and put a new spirit within us. You have the mind of Christ, the heart of a King and the spirit of an overcomer!

God has saved you and called you to His Kingdom to live as a champion! He has prepared you for this day!

Zechariah 12:8

'The weakest among them will be as mighty as King David! And the royal descendants will be like God, like the angel of the Lord who goes before them!'

While in Israel last year, we visited the 'Cave of Elijah'. As I was about to leave, the Lord said to me, *'Don't go without taking something with you'*.

I looked around, and there on the step in the corner was a small white stone.

I picked it up and left with it.

I appreciated that I had something from Elijah's cave, but it took me a while to realise the significance of the 'white stone'. In Revelation, the white stone is given to the overcomer and on it is written a new name.

Revelation 2:17

'But the one whose heart is open let him listen carefully to what the Spirit is presently saying to all the churches. To everyone who is victorious I will let him feast on the hidden manna and give him a shining white stone. And written upon the white stone is inscribed his new name, known only to the one who receives it'.

That stone came from the tomb of Elijah, the ultimate overcomer who turned the heart of Israel back to God. Elijah brought down the prophets of Baal who influenced Israel to turn from their devotion to God and worship other gods. He brought down their authority — he took off their heads! Their voices were silenced in the land and their authority negated.

Elijah ultimately re-established the name of the Lord and returned Israel to the worship of God. The spirit of Elijah turns the hearts of the children to the fathers (Malachi 4:5-6). In Israel, he overcame the power of the enemy and turned the hearts of the children to the Father in Heaven. John the Baptist came in the same spirit of Elijah, turning hearts to the Father again and causing a great repentance. Jesus is coming to the harvest fields and the nations must be prepared. He is waiting on us, His overcomers, to pull down the enemy's strongholds and release the knowledge of the love of the Father, so that the harvest can be reaped.

We have been given this same authority to silence those enemies that speak into our world and influence our lives in negative ways. God is calling us to rise into the fullness of the power and authority the Holy Spirit has given us. He is calling us into our authority as kings and priests to rule and reign in this life.

I believe God has a white stone for us all in this season. It is the authority to 'take out' the influence of the false agenda of the enemy that has ruled your life, the lives of your family, community, city and nation. God has a new name for you, the name of an overcomer.

Ask the Lord what your new overcoming name is!

The most famous of warriors in scripture is David, who overcame Goliath. He had a warrior mentality that would not back down! His faith and courage demanded,

> 'Who is this uncircumcised Philistine that he should defy the armies of the living God?' (1 Samuel 17:26)

In our present-day world, many giants are defying the armies of the living God. Wherever a giant has set himself against you and your family, he is trespassing on land that belongs to God. Wherever he has set himself against the generations, the nations and the land, he has set himself against those Christ died for. You and your family, your city, your generation, your nation, and your land are the inheritance of Jesus upon the earth. Where the enemy is harassing you, he is harassing Jesus. He is defying Jesus!

As always, the Lord will take what the enemy has meant for harm and turn it for His good. God has heard the cries of the oppressed, neglected, and abused peoples of the earth. He has also heard the cries from innocent blood that has been shed and He has stood up to take action!

God Himself just stood up to bring justice to the earth! God has risen up to depose the powers that have kept the peoples in their grasp. The 'gavel of God' has come down in the earth, to judge and overthrow principalities and powers that have perpetuated injustice and suffering.

The enemy of our souls, Satan, has also seen God stand to act. He too has risen, attempting to oppose what God is doing. It reminds me a little of Jesus going to the cross. If the enemy had known what a victory would be won, he would never have killed the Son of God. I believe that God will win a great victory and the enemy will be sorry that he promoted this worldwide disaster. God is going to use it for worldwide revival.

The time of Harvest is now. The time for the healing of the nations is now.

Jesus is our champion of History and we get to write and re-write history as we align ourselves to see *'His Kingdom come and His will done on earth as it is in heaven.'* Do not be phased by the giants that are currently manifesting. They are nothing more than Goliath and his hordes attempting to intimidate the people of God. Rise, in the spirit and courage of David. It is time to arise and declare, 'You come against me with sword and javelin, but I come against you in the Name of the Armies of the Lord of Hosts, against who you stand'.

I heard the Lord say:

Arise and Shine, Nation of God, for the glory of the Lord has risen over you!

Now is the time!

Now is the hour of His Kingdom's glory to be revealed to the nations.

Take up your authority and rule in the midst of your enemies!

Greater is He who is in you than he who is in the world!

His Kingdom is Advancing.

Prepare the Way for the King!

Rise and Shift the Nations!

Knowing that we have the authority to overcome the enemy, we cannot sit back and allow the enemy to harass us and our loved ones. We must rise as David and demand the enemies of our souls, our families, our community and nation to surrender to the power of Heaven!

The Time Is 'NOW'

The prophets in the church and the world media have declared that we have come into a 'New Era'. It is an era so new, it is yet to be named! I would like to believe it will be the Era of Light.

I heard the spirit of God say,

'It is a new Renaissance era. It will be a renaissance of the Book of Acts church and it will transform all sectors of society.'

In fact, I have a sense that, when we look back, today's church will seem to have been in the 'dark ages' in comparison to what we will come into.

The first Renaissance period is widely believed to have begun in Florence, Italy. in the 15th and 16th Century. It is said that it was a convergence of many factors that merged to see a new era emerge:

1. There was political upheaval after the take-over of Greece by the Turks. This meant an influx of many new thinkers and artists had gathered in Florence.

2. The Black Plague had swept through Europe bringing the death of more than one fourth of the population, mostly children.

This caused many to question the status quo and rethink their life on earth. It also meant a change in social demographics.

3. The value of the working class increased as the need for labourers grew, and commoners came to enjoy more freedom.

4. Renaissance authors increasingly began to write. They wrote in vernacular languages and eventually with the introduction of the printing press, this would allow many more people access to books, especially the Bible.

5. This made way in later years for the Reformation to emerge: 'The invention of the printing press by German printer Johannes Gutenberg allowed the rapid transmission of these new ideas. As it spread, the ideas diversified and changed, being adapted to local culture.' [1]

I believe we are coming into a similar time of convergence. The right conditions for great change are appearing together. The culture, the technology, current mindsets and hardships are bringing people to the right place at the right time. The earth is poised, ready to receive the advance of the Kingdom of God.

Any soccer, netball or football game explains this scenario. The teams jostle, attempting to manoeuvre themselves into a position to find an opportune time to take a shot or make the touch down. We are in that opportune time now. Now is the time for the army of God to rise and take this opportunity to bring in the great harvest of the nations. God has brought us to this opportune time, a *kairos* time in the Kingdom.

God brings His people and the world into convergence so that He can orchestrate opportune times for deliverance. When

God brought the children of Israel out of Egypt after 430 years, it was an opportune time. It was in God's timing in history, when He brought all the necessary factors together to set His people free. I believe God has brought us, like the Israelites, to the edge of the promised land, and He is encouraging His people again to rise up and possess their inheritance.

Throughout scripture, when God brings in a time of deliverance to establish a New Era, He raises up an army to enforce it on the earth. Any kingdom that advances, advances with an army. Armies exist firstly for the protection of the kingdom or nation and secondly, for the advancing of the nation to possess territories and kingdoms they wish to subdue. The Kingdom of God is no different.

When Israel came out of Egypt under the leadership of Moses, the children of Israel came forth into the new era as an army.[2] In the days of Joshua, the warriors were drawn into battle array to again bring forth a new era. They went into the land as an army to take their promises.[3] When Jesus was born into the earth, He came with His army. Thousands and thousands of the hosts of heavens armies. All singing 'Glory to God in the highest!' [4]

The Hosts Of Heaven's Armies Is Captained By Jesus Christ Himself.

Revelation 19:11-14

'Then I saw heaven opened, and suddenly a white horse appeared. The name of the one riding it was Faithful and True, and with pure righteousness he judges and rides to battle. He wore many regal crowns, his eyes were flashing like flames of fire. He had a secret name inscribed on him that's known only to himself. He wore a robe dipped in blood, and his title is called the Word of God. Following him on white horses were the armies of heaven, wearing white fine linen, pure and bright'.

For 40 years, the Israelites were destined to wander in the wilderness because they failed to believe they were great warriors in God's Kingdom who were able to possess the promised land. They were intimidated by the enemy and refused to fight and therefore missed living in their promised land. This has been a warning for every person and generation since Jesus' victory. On the cross, Jesus delivered us from all the power of the enemy. His promise is that we, also, through faith in His complete victory and authority, fight to live in the fullness of the Kingdom.

However, God offered the Israelites another 'opportune time' to take hold of the promised land and they rose up as an army, ready to fight. The Israelites took the promised land and went from being ruled by powers of darkness and idol worship, to a land ruled under God. Ultimately, in Solomon's era, Israel displayed the abundant blessings that come to a nation that lives under God's standards and principles. [5]

An Army To Bless The Nations

The abundant blessings of living in God's Kingdom on earth continued to be displayed as the first apostles introduced the then known world to the love and power of the gospel. The gospel of the first century church gained so much momentum that it changed the landscape of nations.

Throughout Asia Minor and Greece and even into Rome, the gospel changed the way people lived. Temples made to honour Greek gods were converted to churches. Churches grew up all around the regions and the church flourished and expanded. By the time of the rule of Constantine, Christianity became the official religion of the known world.[6] Although, after this took place, the influence of the gospels was lost, early Christian history displays the willingness in the heart of God and the power of His gospel to transform nations.

Historians say that the Wesleyan Revival of the 1700s spared England from revolution. Not only were people's hearts and mindsets changed, the understanding of the righteousness and justice of God meant great social reform. The age of child labour was increased, workers' hours were reduced, and among many other things, the slave trade in England was abolished.

Revelation 11:15

'Then the seventh angel blew his trumpet, and there were loud voices shouting in heaven:
'The world has now become the Kingdom of our Lord and of his Christ, and he will reign forever and ever'".

Today, for the church of Jesus Christ to rise and shine and possess the promises for ourselves and the nations, it is vital to understand what it is to be a warrior.

It is necessary that the body of Christ today be trained as the army that we are, and that we rise to live in the promises Jesus says are ours. The enemy's agenda has been dominating the landscape in the nations. This is especially true in the west in nations that once declared themselves to be Christian. Since the 1960s, many western nations have systematically had their Judaeo-Christian based legal system eroded. The church has not had the power to overcome the world nor the authority to show the world a way out of the dilemmas being faced on so many levels.

Now, in this era, Jesus, who has won the kingdoms of this world, is calling us to rise into the army. With a warrior mindset, we can take hold of the promises He has given to us and to the world now. God is offering a new generation, along with those from the previous generation still in faith, an 'opportune time' to rise up again. It's an opportunity to fight to possess fullness of life for our families, communities and nations.

God is again empowering His people to rise in authority to shift and change nations. We are His people whom He has empowered to display the works of the Father. God is looking for a generation who are strong and will do exploits. He is calling for a Joshua generation who will rise up by faith and take hold of His promises at this opportune time! It is time for the church of Jesus Christ to Rise and Shine!

I heard the Lord say:

Yes, it is no longer business as usual; you have broken into a whole new realm of My Kingdom come into the earth!

It is My good pleasure to give to you the Kingdom!

It's alive and fresh, just like the dawning of the new day!

It's spectacular in its potential,

It's unprecedented in its favour,

It's miraculous in its access to the power of the throne of Heaven!

It's unparalleled in its beauty, the beauty it will bring to the earth through my people who know me and love me and have poured out their lives to see my Kingdom come!

It's spectacular in its significance, for this new realm of glory upon the earth has the potential to usher in the great end time harvest!

Don't be weary in well doing! I have called you to even greater dimensions of the knowledge of the glory of the Lord upon the earth, and it is you, my faithful warriors, whom I have called to continue to fight the good fight of faith and see my Kingdom advance in the earth!

My army, my triumphant reserve, is the greatest force in the earth!

Rise in the authority I have given you in these last days, for the advancing of My Kingdom in the earth rests upon your shoulders.

Yes, I have anointed you and empowered you as the 'mighty men' of David's army and as David did, I trust you with My life!

Today, I anoint you for glory!

The glory realm will be your portion and your inheritance!

Today, I anoint you to life!

Today, I anoint you with the power and authority of heaven displayed in unprecedented ways upon the earth!

God has brought us again to an 'opportune time' in history to see the church rise in her overcoming power and become a powerful force throughout the nations for righteousness and justice!

Jesus and His hosts are fighting alongside us to enforce the finished work of the cross. He died so that the earth and her people could return to the knowledge of the love of the Father.

CHAPTER 2

Revelations to Advance the Kingdom of Heaven in the Nations

The body of Christ moves with the Holy Spirit to receive fresh revelation to continue to advance the Kingdom of God in the earth. There have been a number of major revelations concerning the body of Christ that have emerged in past decades. These fresh revelations are enabling the body of Christ to move forward into this New Era. In fact, these revelations are producing a new wineskin for the people of God, so that the 'new wine' that God has promised in the New Era will not be lost for future generations.

These new paradigm shifts release the people of God to effectively enforce the Kingdom of God's rule and leadership in the earth.

In fact, I heard the Lord say:

In this New Era of Enlightenment or Lights, the light of Christ will again become the dominating influence upon the earth.

The parameters are set, and further revelation will flow in abundance to ensure that the impact of My Kingdom will continue strong in the earth.

It is My day of deliverance and My time to reveal again the great 'I AM' upon the earth.

I will fulfil all the prophecies of My Book. I AM raising up a people who will rightly divide My word, understand and pray with Heaven, joining forces, so that the earth will know that the God of Glory has come again with great salvation for all.

In the last 70 years, God has released new revelation to the body of Christ. These new revelations have helped develop new wineskins for the people of God. These new mindsets and operating systems are essential to ensure that the church is able to catch and flourish on the new wine that the Lord is about to pour out in the earth.

1. The Foundation of Righteousness and Justice

God declares that righteousness and justice are the firm foundations of His throne.

Psalm 89:14
'Righteousness and justice are the foundation of your throne. Unfailing love and truth walk before you as attendants'.

The Kingdom of God on earth will be established in the same way; on a foundation of righteousness and justice. The throne and government of God is from eternity to eternity. If God's throne, built on righteousness and justice, is sustained for eternity, then our lives, families and the nations will also be established and flourish when also built on righteousness and justice.

Scripture declares that rulers and those in authority will be established and have longevity when they rule in righteousness and justice. This is the way that God rules in His Kingdom, and this is then the best way to rule the nations.

Proverbs 14:34
'A nation is exalted by the righteousness of its people, but sin heaps disgrace upon the land'.

Proverbs 29:2 (NLT)
'When the godly are in authority, the people rejoice. But when the wicked are in power, they groan'.

Jesus died so that we as individuals, communities and peoples across the earth could be established in righteousness. This righteousness brings access to abundant and eternal life. When we govern our lives by continuing to submit to the righteousness that Jesus has established us in, we prosper in every area of our lives. God's Word overflows with references to the benefits of living in righteousness. [1]

> Psalm 106:3 (TPT)
> 'The happiest one on earth is the one who keeps your word and clings to righteousness every moment'.

> Psalm 72:3 (TPT)
> 'Then the mountains of influence will be fruitful, and from your righteousness, prosperity and peace will flow to all the people'.

Righteousness is the plumb line from which God governs His Kingdom. As such, it is also the plumb line by which He governs the earth and its people. From individuals to nations, those who govern their world by the plumb line of righteousness will find strength and security.

When righteousness laws are eroded away and justice is compromised, nations will crumble from the inside out. It has been true in history and it is true in western nations today. Revolution is man's way of attaining justice when injustice has prevailed. However, man's way will not bring a nation to justice. Instead, it often merely transfers the injustice onto another group of people.

> Isaiah 59:14
> 'Justice is driven away and righteousness stands on the sidelines, for truth has stumbled in the public square and morality cannot enter'.

Justice is measured out from the plumb line of righteousness. Without righteousness as our plumb line, we cannot determine real justice. Unless the laws of the nations are established in the righteous parameters outlined in Scripture, justice will be impossible to secure in the nations.

Isaiah 28:17
'I will test you with the measuring line of justice and the plumb line of righteousness'.

God is a God of justice, and He is also a God of peace. For peace to prevail, justice must be issued. To issue justice, someone must make a judgement. Justice must be served. It must be upheld. Injustice cannot be tolerated in the land, as history demonstrates.

Isaiah 32:17
'The work of righteousness is peace, and the result of righteousness is quietness and confidence forever'.

Jesus fulfilled all righteousness and now justice is delivered on earth through faith in the blood of Jesus, by the forces of heaven, for heaven now has full access to earth.

Where justice is established on earth through the blood of Jesus and the release of the armies of heaven, God uses His people on earth. The people of God, with the power of the Holy Spirit and the angel armies, apply the overcoming power of the blood of the Lamb by faith. This gives the people of God authority to shift the spiritual and subsequently the natural realm into alignment with the will of the Father. As such, the justice of

God can be established through the power of the blood, where the power of the blood and forgiveness is evoked by faith.[3]

Where the power of the blood is rejected by people and the pathway of forgiveness is rejected, then God in His goodness will continue to establish justice in the earth through His forces on the earth. God is a good God who hears the cries of the oppressed and downtrodden, and He will NOT allow the oppressor to continue in his oppression.

> Romans 12:19
>
> 'Beloved, don't be obsessed with taking revenge, but leave that to God's righteous justice. For the Scriptures say: "If you don't take justice in your own hands, I will release justice for you," says the Lord'".

The God of all justice is long-suffering, patient and kind and He sees that wounded humanity continues to wound itself. He hears the cries of the poor, downtrodden and neglected, and He is close to the broken-hearted. He has sent Jesus as the saviour to answer humanity's crisis. Jesus has made a way in the earth so that God no longer needs to use the powers within the earth to establish justice for the oppressed but all can be freely forgiven.

Enforcing Righteousness And Justice

Army of God, Arise! God has called and equipped His people to bring righteousness and justice into the earth through the power of Jesus' blood and the word of our testimony. With the hosts of Heaven's army, the Lord Himself will captain His people into a just and righteous world.

Jesus has made available to His warriors on earth a full arsenal of weapons. Through faith, we are able to enforce the rule and reign of Jesus into every corner of the globe. We have the privilege of hearing Jesus' strategies in the earth and joining the armies of heaven to enforce the advancement of the Kingdom of Heaven on earth. God has a strategy for every individual, family, community and nation. The Lord does not wish that any should perish but for all to have everlasting life![4]

> Proverbs 31:8-9
> 'But you are to be a king who speaks up on behalf of the disenfranchised and pleads for the legal rights of the defenceless and those who are dying.
> 'Be a righteous king, judging on behalf of the poor and interceding for those most in need'.

As kings and priests that serve our God, and as warriors in the earth, we are called to rise and administer justice from heaven to earth. This can be done through prophetic words and decrees by faith in the power of the blood that establishes righteousness.

> Isaiah 32:1
> 'Look—a New Era begins! A king will reign with righteousness, and his princes according to justice!'

The nations of the world, as well as the modern-day church, are caught in the oppression of the world system. Like as in

Egypt, we are oppressed by the worship of Baal, which is the greed of the world system and the basis for almost every sin. There is also the oppression of ISIS. This was another major Egyptian God at the time of Israel's captivity. This god required child sacrifice. These evil spirits have again risen on the world stage, empowered by the shedding of innocent blood across the nations.

The nations that have previously lived by the laws and standards of the Bible are swiftly changing their righteous laws, giving way to the ever-encroaching deceptions of the enemy. The demands of those who have chosen to run after the greed and deception of these dominating world powers are plunging the nations into chaos, strife and further injustice and oppression.

I believe that the Lord has seen the oppression and He has heard the cries of humanity across the nations. He has heard the cries of those caught in unjust, oppressive situations, those persecuted in ungodly nations, those enslaved by perverse lifestyles, and those aborted before their time. He is coming to again display His power in the earth.

The power of Jesus as Lord will again be powerfully displayed in the earth on behalf of the poor and oppressed. He will come through His people, the church. He will cause faith and authority and His overcoming power to be seen through His people! His heart and will are to pour out His love and freedom upon the earth, so that all will know the Father and His goodness and turn and be healed.

It is time for the full revelation of the authority of the

Lordship of Christ in the earth, as it was in the time of Jesus. The Lord wants His glory revealed, so all will know that the Lord Jesus is the Lord of all the earth! It is time for the Kingdom of Heaven to be seen across the nations so that His people and nations are released into the promises of His covenant.

Never doubt the love of the Father, Son and Holy Spirit. God declares that His glory will cover the earth, as the waters cover the sea. That glory was made known to Moses. He asked God, 'Show me your glory'. God responded that He would allow His goodness to pass before Him. God's glory and goodness are one and the same. God is raising up His people and sending us out to display His goodness across the nations, to all people.

God is causing His power and authority to be seen in greater ways through His people, who are to exercise the delivering power of Jesus throughout the nations.

Luke 2:14

'Glory to God in the highest realms of heaven!
For there is peace and a good hope given to the sons of men.'

2. The Revelation of the Church as the Ekklesia

Jesus addressed Peter in Matthew 16:18

'I give you the name Peter, a stone. And this truth of who I am will be the bedrock foundation on which I will build my church (ekklesia)—my legislative assembly, and the power of death will not be able to overpower it!'

The word 'church' in this passage is translated from the Greek work 'ekklesia.'

The 'ekklesia' of the Roman and Greek empires, however, was nothing like our churches of today. The ekklesia that Jesus spoke of was a ruling assembly of citizens in the Grecian democracy that governed its city states. The Romans assimilated the concept and the ekklesia became a body of people assembled to conduct governmental business and enforce the laws and cultural ways of the Roman empire in the nations they conquered. [5]

When we understand the concept of the ekklesia, we then understand that Christ has called His church to be an assembly of people who use their legislative power in the heavenly realm to enforce a culture of His Kingdom rule on the earth. Jesus asked us to pray, 'on earth, as it is in heaven.' Therefore, it is our privilege and call to embrace this mandate to transform communities and nations.

The mandate of the church is not to blend into society, but to be a catalyst for the love of the Father and the ways of His Kingdom rule to invade the earth. This will enable people to experience life and life abundantly! Understanding the church as the ekklesia defines how the church can advance the Kingdom of Heaven on earth. It will take a continuing shift of mindset for the body of Christ to rise up as the people of God, with His authority to enforce the culture of the Kingdom of Heaven on earth.

Ed Silvoso in his book, *Ekklesia: Rediscovering God's Instrument for Global Transformation* says,

> Jesus did not state, 'I will build my temple or I will build my synagogue', the two most prominent religious institutions at the time. Instead, he chose a secular entity first developed by the Greeks when He said, 'I will build my ekklesia!' [6]

It is no longer acceptable for the church to be viewed and treated simply as another sector of society fulfilling the role of serving the community in the way the community will allow. The true calling of the church of Jesus Christ is to shift in the heavens, the principalities and powers restraining the Kingdom of God, and release communities, cites and nations in the spiritual realm, so that Heaven on earth can be experienced in every sector of society.

Our authority in the earth begins with our authority in the heavens. Jesus very clearly states to His disciples that His Kingdom is not of this world. He declares that His Kingdom is a spiritual Kingdom and it is this Kingdom that we are advancing in the earth.[7] However, like Jesus, we advance His Kingdom in the spiritual realm and then it is demonstrated in the natural realm, in a shift of nations into righteousness, peace and joy.

3. The Authority of the Ekklesia – Knowing our identity and authority as sons and daughters of God

The immense love of the Father towards His people and all

of creation is again being believed and received by the people of God. The understanding of our identity as sons and daughters of God and all that means is coming into greater focus.

Revelation knowledge of what it means to have God as a Father has led the body of Christ to understand relationship based on His unconditional love, rather than fear or duty; or only knowing Him through the often flawed reflection of earthly fathers. Understanding 'who we are and whose we are', produces a relationship of unshakeable security and unconditional love.

In this knowledge, we rise in faith and live in the higher law of love, not just the law of Moses, that demands we must legalistically follow the rules. There is a new-found freedom of joy and peace, knowing that God really is interested in each individual and wants to meet every need. There is a new-found acceptance, confidence and faith, knowing He is cheering His people on to succeed.

The knowledge of who we are and whose we are builds a confidence that is fashioning a people who are bold in love to demonstrate the Father's goodness. As Bill Johnson says, 'We move from intimacy with God, to identity in God, to the authority of God.' In this, we rise in faith to be overcomers for ourselves, our families and our nations.

Relationship with the Father, Son and Holy Spirit gives His sons and daughters the authority to advance the Kingdom. As children of God, we are called to grow in maturity in the knowledge and understanding of the ways of our Father. As we mature into adulthood, our relationship with our natural parents shifts most often to one of friendship. The same is true with God. Our relationship can progress from child of God to becoming a friend of God.

Scripture tells us that God shares His secrets with His friends. We know Moses was a friend of God.[8] As we become a friend of God, He will share His concerns and desires for the nations with us. When we understand God's desire and will for the nations, like Moses we can intercede and make a difference in the earth.

As such, our real focus then, must be on becoming a friend of God. Friends spend time together, sharing fellowship, concerns, and love. Those who are worshippers of God, who know God in prayer and friendship, will rise with an authority and warrior spirit to overcome the enemy and enforce God's desire in their sphere of influence.

Romans 8:19-21

'The entire universe is standing on tiptoe, yearning to see the unveiling of God's glorious sons and daughters! For against its will the universe itself has had to endure the empty futility resulting from the consequences of human sin. But now, with eager expectation, all creation longs for freedom from its slavery to decay and to experience with us the wonderful freedom coming to God's children.'

The church is being called to rise and shine.[9] God has prepared His bride to be a people who will stand to display the love of the Father throughout the nations. He is fashioning a generation who knows the authority that the Father has given them to invade every sector of society to establish the righteous and just ways of the Kingdom.

God is putting an *'axe to the root of the tree'* of unjust and oppressive ways throughout the nations of the earth! He is doing this through a people who will rise in their identity and authority as God's sons and daughters and be His ambassadors on the earth! He is calling forth sons and daughters to be change agents in the nations.

To shift and change culture in this way requires a people with an overcoming mindset that will pull down the enemy's plans and establish the Kingdom, in the power of the Spirit.

CHAPTER 3

More Revelations to Advance the Kingdom of Heaven in the Nations

1. The 7-Mountain Mandate Mindset to Facilitate Societal Change

The 7 Mountain revelation gives understanding of how to shift nations by influencing every sector of society.

Dr. Bill Bright and Loren Cunningham, as statesmen of the church, were both given revelation concerning the 7 Mountains of culture. Their understanding is that if Christ's mandate to disciple nations is to be fulfilled, then the church of Jesus Christ must engage with all 7 sectors of society. We cannot see the earth transformed to be like heaven without changing and influencing every facet of the world we live in.[1]

In recent generations, the church of Jesus Christ has been diligent to send missionaries into nations with the hope that as individuals were saved *en masse*, a whole nation would change and shift their operating systems under the Lordship of Christ. However, as Cindy Jacobs explains in her book, '*The Reformation Manifesto*', getting people saved does not necessarily translate to a shift of society under the Lordship of Christ. She gives the example of her home state of Texas. She says roughly 80% of people declare that they are Christians and yet the crime and murder rate is as high as any other state in America.[2]

Recently, while listening to a broadcast from Glory of Zion, I heard a Nigerian pastor speak. He told the story of how one of their pastors asked a Christian leader from the West not to bring any more crusades to her nation. She explained that 90% of the people in her nation say they are Christians, and yet the nation is full of lawlessness, cruelty and crime. She asked that someone come and make a real difference in the crushing statistics of crime, poverty and murder that are crippling the country.[3]

These facts highlight the need to bring change to the whole framework of society. The church of Jesus Christ is now recognising that nations must be discipled not only with salvation for individuals but through biblical righteousness and justice established in every sector of society. When this happens, we will see nations truly operate under the principles and peace of the Kingdom of Heaven.

When Jesus spoke of salvation, He used the Greek word,

'Sozo', which translates to 'abundant life, nothing missing, and nothing broken'. Jesus' promise of salvation was not just to individuals but to the nations. [4a,b]

2. The Five-Fold Government of God Empowering the Church to Facilitate Societal Change.

In 2008, Peter Wagner wrote the book, *Dominion! How Kingdom Action Can Change the World*. He wrote that Jesus has mandated His church to actively engage in transforming society on earth by fulfilling Matthew 6:10: *'Thy kingdom come on earth as it is in heaven'*. [5]

Dr. Wagner then shared how the church could rise in their governing authority to realise this shift of Kingdom culture. Through the re-establishing of the role of the five-fold ministries as the governmental authority in the church, the church can be re-aligned and equipped to be the catalyst for change and transformation in the nations.

These five-fold leaders carry authority in the church, and also in society across the seven mountains, cities, nations and internationally.[6]

Paul in 1 Corinthians 12:28 says,

'Here are some of the parts God has appointed for the church: first are apostles, second are prophets, third are teachers, then those who do miracles, those who have the gift of healing, those who can help others, those who have the gift of leadership, those who speak in unknown languages'.

In the early church, it was the apostles and the five-fold who were given governing authority to organise the church to operate effectively in the 'new era' in which they found themselves. The apostles of the early church governed and expanded the church through apostolic hubs in the cities of Asia Minor. Paul was the apostle who evangelised, gathered and started many of the churches. He then oversaw them, discipled them and went back to visit them often.

God is re-establishing the five-fold as the governing power for the body of Christ so that the church can again powerfully advance in discipling and transforming nations. The modern-day apostle has authority to gather the body of Christ together to see the church come into unity and move the Kingdom of God forward in the nations. A recent example we see in the past American elections. Franklin Graham called church members to pray, to run for office and to vote.[7] His authority called the Christians of America together in unity for a common purpose. Shift and change have been happening in and through America ever since.

There are also prophets being raised up who not only prophesy in their churches or church events, but who God is positioning with leaders of nations. The leaders are listening to the voice of the prophets. It is understood that Paula White is currently a prophetic voice and advisor to the former American president, Donald Trump.[8] Leaders want to hear what God is saying and what God wants for their nations.

Reinhard Bonnke was a great example of an evangelist with the authority of a five-fold minister who was able to carry

Christ into nations across Africa. He had authority to call the body of Christ together to see shift and change. In December 2019, Bonnke passed into glory, having had 79 million people respond to his gospel message.[9]

Other five-fold ministers are being raised up across the 7 Mountains in the form of governmental leaders. These leaders operate in the authority of apostles, prophets, pastors, teachers and evangelists in their sphere of influence. As political and business leaders, they are operating to bring righteousness and wealth to nations. God has raised up some as legislators to bring justice into their sphere of influence. The understanding of the authority of the five-fold ministry in the church and in the other mountains of society is beginning to emerge to bring the possibility of transformation to nations.

The Foundational Role Of The Apostle And Prophet

Ephesians 2:20 says that the church is built on the foundation of the apostle and prophet.

> 'You are rising like the perfectly fitted stones of the temple; and your lives are being built up together upon the ideal foundation laid by the apostles and prophets, and best of all, you are connected to the Head Cornerstone of the building, the Anointed One, Jesus Christ himself!'

God is raising up His apostles and prophets and bringing them together as the governmental authority in the church today. This powerful combination is God's divine strategy to deliver nations, transform and disciple them. In Scripture, the visual of Moses and Aaron walking together gives a 'pre-church era' picture of the apostle and prophet walking together to deliver and disciple a nation.

Although there was no language for it, Moses and Aaron appear to be operating in the foundational gift of the apostle and prophet:

1. They gave power-filled leadership that firstly delivered the people of God out of bondage.
2. They used their governmental authority to put people in position and order, so that as an army, they were effective in battle.
3. They established the nation into a people of worship who carried the presence of God among them.
4. Moses had governmental authority to organise the people to live under righteous laws that ensured justice and fairness throughout the nation.

In Exodus 6:10-13, Moses and Aaron, the apostle and prophet, work together to shift the people of God into their rightful position in the nations. Apostles and prophets today will have many of the same characteristics that Moses and Aaron had.

Like Moses, the apostle will not trust in their own strength, but they will be totally dependent on God, and in unity with the prophet, God leads them to function alongside. They may have obvious faults, but they will be 'called' and 'empowered' by God. Like Moses and Aaron, they will have a pedigree in the Spirit and will have been raised by faith-filled fathers and mothers. These may not be natural fathers and mothers, but like Joshua, they will be sons and daughters of faith.

Some, like Moses, will have been trained in the world, but will also have been trained through the hard places of the 'desert times'. Like Aaron, others will have been trained in the house of God among the people of God, yet they will understand the harshness of the world system. God will raise them up with the 'word of the Lord' for the body of Christ and for the rulers and leaders in the nations.

They will be obedient to speak all that the Lord commands them to speak in all humility and grace. We know that Moses was called the humblest man that ever lived. The main characteristic of leaders who God raises up to deliver nations is that they are men known for their humility before God and others.

Across the body of Christ today, God is bringing apostolic and prophetic leaders together with the express purpose of bringing the body of Christ into the fullness of her inheritance and call. This call is the same as the call on Israel, the first peoples of God. It is a call to embrace an inheritance in the nations, so that all the peoples of the earth will be blessed. The people of God under apostolic leaders can be equipped to be a people that call others out of oppression and into possession and promise.

How Apostles And Prophets Operate In The Church Today

Ephesians 4:11-12 (TPT) says,

'And he has appointed some with grace to be apostles, and some with grace to be prophets, and some with grace to be evangelists, and some with grace to be pastors, and some with grace to be teachers.

'And their calling is to nurture and prepare all the holy believers to do their own works of ministry, and as they do this they will enlarge and build up the body of Christ'.

In the last 20 years, the body of Christ has been learning how the 'apostles and prophets' are to be activated and operate in the body. As the role of the apostle and prophet and the whole five-fold offices are understood and released, an effective governing body of Christ is emerging across the church today. The purpose is to release the people of God to effectively bring shift and change to the nations. The effective discipling of nations.

Scripture says that the body of Christ operates as a family. This simple analogy helps to understand how the apostle and prophet operate as foundational to church government. The apostle and prophet could be compared to the parents of a family. [10]

Every family has a heritage and an inheritance. The apostles and prophets and the whole five-fold exist to 'equip' the body, to grow and be established to fulfil their destiny. The five-fold parent the new and emerging leaders and allow them to come forth into all they are called to. Just like any growing family, the parents delight to see the young adults flourishing and doing better than they ever did. It is the delight of the parents to see the new generation take their place and become the ones who carry the generations forward. They go on to produce children, and now, as fathers, equip and train these children. The apostolic grandparents act as the foundation that holds together the whole family.

As stressed previously, the apostle and prophet are called the foundations of the church with Jesus Christ the chief cornerstone. They are set at the base of the structure. So in this analogy of family, they serve the next generation by nurturing and fathering them into righteousness, peace and joy. The foundations give a sure footing and firm foundation on which the next generation can stand. Thus, the role of the Apostle and Prophet in the church is much like the role of the grandparent in the family.

Initially, the parent raises and is responsible for everything the child needs in their development. The parents are the mainstay of the home. They provide for the family. They give guidance, nurture encouragement direction and discipline, until the children grow.

When the child grows, they find their own interest and passion and call of God for their lives. When this happens, the loving parent releases and encourages but continues to support the upcoming generation to fulfil their dreams. This loving parent allows the next generation to take up their responsibility. The parents pass on the baton as this next generation now births and nurtures another generation.

The now loving grandparent always stays connected, offering advice when asked and making suggestions that may or may not be followed. However, a loving, cooperative, encouraging supportive relationship is always maintained to encourage, empower and help.

Another supporting analogy regarding the role of the apostle and prophet as foundational, is that of a huge tree, in which the root structure holds and causes the whole tree to flourish and give fruit. This root system ensures the tree is firmly established and positioned to receive the nutrients needed to pass onto the ever-growing new shoots of the tree. It provides nourishment and stability for the new branches to be established and holds them up so that they in turn produce new branches.

This is the joy of the apostles and prophets. They do not lord it over others, but they undergird, encourage and nurture the upcoming leaders, so that the tree flourishes.

This is how the body of Christ is to function. It is like the growing and maturing of a tree. The five-fold is the root system giving support and strength to allow the next generation of leaders to follow the call of God. The ever-growing tree flourishes and produces fruit and then provides shade and a home to all who come to live under its branches.

Shifting Culture Through Generational Impact

When apostles and prophets, along with the rest of the five-fold (pastors, teachers and evangelists) function together in this way, the people of God will become a healthy family, lovingly connected and supportive of one another. The rising generation will feel supported and will be given room to grow and flourish. In this way, the ever-emerging generations will remain in relationship to their heritage, all the while receiving an inheritance.

The five-fold are simply the parenting body, who love and grow the children of God to adulthood. They are now equipped and more importantly released to flourish and fulfil the destiny of their own lives. When this happens down several generations, the children come into their destiny which can become a dynasty.

A dynasty established down the generations has power to influence the culture and prosperity of the nations. There are many great examples of this across the nations and generations both in the body of Christ and in business enterprises. In scripture we see Timothy, who was mighty in the land because of his heritage of faith. In England we see the Salvation Army that continued after the death of William and Catherine Booth because of the legacy through their children. In the business and political arena, the Rockefeller empire continues down the generations. The Kennedy Dynasty has steered the nation of America in the past and continues to have influence.

There is great hope for the body of Christ if we can disciple the next generation into faith. It is not an easy thing and rarely seen in scripture. However when three generations align with a common faith, we see God establish and shift nations.

Through the faith and continued vision of Abraham, Isaac and Jacob, a nation was born. Through the transfer of faith from Moses' mother, to Moses to Joshua, the nation of Israel were re-established in the land of their promises. This same pattern was used as Samuel anointed and nurtured David, who passed his faith to Solomon, who rose to bring Israel into a 'golden era.'

This same pattern was even needed for the establishing of the new era church through Jesus. John the Baptist made a way, Jesus was the way, and the church of Jesus Christ was established through the faith of Peter and the apostles. God has much more in store for His body as we train the generations and pass on the baton of faith in such a way that future generations complete their course.

A New Era Of His Power

The Importance Of Understanding We Are Now In A New Era

We have entered a New Era and it is an appointed time to move forward and take possession of all that God has promised. God is calling His people to rise and shine. Now is the time to rise again and take hold of His promises for the nations.

However, to embrace the new, there is often a corresponding letting go of the old. Change, by definition, is not comfortable. It is a process that confronts our established position and demands adjustment.

The Renaissance and the Reformation did not emerge without struggle and push back. In fact; no new period of history has emerged without a wrestle and sometimes even war, to see 'the new' come to birth.

History shows us just how costly it has been for many who have stood and declared their conviction that it was time to enter the new era. There are many heroes down the generations who rose to proclaim the dream for a new way that God had put in their heart. Many even lost their lives for it.

The comfortable 'status quo' will stubbornly resist change. Many will tell you to be quiet and sit down and not rock the boat! Many will be threatened and resist if they think they will lose something, not realising there is so much more to gain. Don't sit down - stand up and rock the boat! We may not all be called to change the world, but we are all called to impact our sphere of influence for the Kingdom.

It may cost you everything you have and who you are. For Jesus, it cost him everything to bring a new era into the earth. It was not the Jews who killed Jesus; it was the religious and traditional spirit over the leaders who were threatened and felt in danger of losing their own privileges. However, this was and still is the only way to bring NEW LIFE to the people of God and to the earth!

To rise and enforce a new era takes courage! It takes those with a different spirit. It takes those with a spirit of Caleb and Joshua! It takes those men and women who have known and seen the power of God displayed! Those who have been trained through the wilderness, those who are now wiser yet still ready to go in and possess their inheritance.

It is imperative that the Joshua and Caleb generation rise again. The next generation need their maturity and leadership skills, so that they are not assigned again to wilderness living.

It will take courage and boldness and not backing down. God Himself is doing the equipping! These are days of deliverance and days of fire!

> Exodus 6:8-9
>
> "'I will bring you into the land I swore to give to Abraham, Isaac, and Jacob. I will give it to you as your very own possession. I am the Lord!" So Moses told the people of Israel what the Lord had said, but they refused to listen anymore. They had become too discouraged by the brutality of their slavery'.

Many may feel they have been too beaten up by the wilderness years to have courage to rise again. When God asked Joshua to lead the people and again go and take possession of the land, He gave him a way to move forward. Today, as the army of God we can use these same steps to rise again and take possession of our inheritance.

CHAPTER FOUR

How Joshua Enforced a New Era

It is imperative that the Joshua and Caleb generation rise again. It takes the fathers and mothers of the generation to help the generations in their care to rise out of the wilderness place and into their inheritance. The next generation needs their maturity and leadership skills, so that they are not assigned again to wilderness living. It will take courage and boldness and not backing down. God Himself is doing the equipping! These are days of deliverance and days of fire!

> Exodus 6:8-9
>
> "'I will bring you into the land I swore to give to Abraham, Isaac, and Jacob. I will give it to you as your very own possession. I am the Lord!" So Moses told the people of Israel what the Lord had said, but they refused to listen anymore. They had become too discouraged by the brutality of their slavery'.

What an absolutely amazing promise and word from the Lord to the people of Israel. Yet they were unable to receive it because the oppression they were under was so harsh.

I believe there are many who are beaten down and so oppressed by their circumstance, they are finding it hard to hear or act on the word to 'Rise and Shine!'

As a body of Christ we have cried out for many years for the promises of God to be made manifest. We have fought many fights, had many struggles, and in many areas we have not seen what we have believed for. We have struggled and still struggle with sickness and disease in our bodies; we have seen families broken and children walk away from faith.

With disappointments and discouragements, it may seem hard to believe again. Israel had 430 years of failed promises, but eventually, it was TIME!

Bruce, my husband, often quotes the late Peter Wagner as saying that he, '...had been on the edge of 7 new moves of God throughout his lifetime and to step into each one, took courage'!

I believe it took courage for the people of Israel to take up their faith again and believe the promise that God gave them through Moses. It takes courage to take step up and believe again. However, it is time to take up our courage and step forward again to where God is calling us, regardless of past performances.

Peter stepped out and sank, but Jesus rescued him. You may have needed rescuing before now, but don't let it stop you from stepping out of the boat again.

It is always time to step out in faith! I believe we will see the goodness of the Lord in the land of the living! It's time! He is coming to deliver His people and His nations in greater measure than we have even expected. He is about to do even more than we can imagine.

When God asked Joshua to rise and lead the people of Israel to take possession of the land, He gave him a word of preparation for himself and the people. Today, as the army of God, we can use these same steps to rise again and take possession of our inheritance.

a) Be strong and very courageous. (Joshua 1:6)[1]

Boldness and courage are essential to any new project. To anyone who has had to begin something new, especially something that has not been done before, it takes boldness and courage. There are great promises God has made to us; we cannot shrink back in this new era. God is encouraging His people to 'go up' into the new land. There are many 'new' things to be done in 'new' ways that are very unfamiliar to us. Boldness and courage is the only way we can walk into the new!

Joshua heard the word of the Lord, but he had to 'act' on it. When the people of Israel did not act on the word God gave Moses, it had massive consequence for a whole nation. Joshua was not going to make the same mistake. We cannot say, 'No', when God says, 'Now'. I believe we can ask the Lord to empower us with courage to launch forward into the new thing he has asked of us.

b) Be careful to obey all the instructions Moses gave you, Do not deviate from them, turning either to the left or the right. (v.7) (1a)

Obedience in everything God is saying is essential. We do not always see the whole picture. Those things we may consider insignificant, may be major issues from God's perspective. It is important to treat very carefully what we hear from heaven. God's few words can open a whole chapter of ideas and insight for the things ahead.

c) Meditate always on the Word of God. (v. 8) (2)

In the new era, with the increase of evil, I believe we must reiterate the importance of knowing the word of the Lord individually as well as the truth of the Word. The world is believing more and more of the lies of the enemy. Many are deceived and cannot discern good and evil. It is necessary for the body of Christ to be well taught in the Word of God and the Spirit of the Word, to ensure we live in the truth and follow the ways of God. Jesus Himself says in the last days many deceptions and doctrines of demons will be in the earth. Understanding this, and knowing the Word and the Spirit of the Word, is therefore vital.

d) No wonder our hearts have melted in fear! (2:9-11)

"'I know the Lord has given you this land,' she told them. "We are all afraid of you. Everyone in the land is living in terror. For we have heard how the Lord made a dry path for you through the Red Sea when you left

Egypt. And we know what you did to Sihon and Og, the two Amorite kings east of the Jordan River, whose people you completely destroyed. No wonder our hearts have melted in fear! No one has the courage to fight after hearing such things. For the Lord your God is the supreme God of the heavens above and the earth below'".

We need to no longer fear the giants. The giants are afraid of us. When the enemy is creating chaos at every turn, you can be sure He is afraid of what God is about to do through you. The giants have seen the power of our God. We need only remind them of Jesus' death and resurrection.

We can know that when we stand up, the enemy cowers. At times, we as Christians have often been in 'defence' mode. We have waited for the enemy to attack and then tried to overcome him. However, the tide has turned. God is calling His body to rise with Him against His enemy. It is the enemy who is now afraid. Do not cower at his futile attempts to intimidate. It is a new day of faith.

We are moving forward with all eyes on Jesus, supremely confident He will take care of us. God is empowering His people with 'hope' at this time! We can rejoice; God is on the move and He is going before us.

Joshua sent in spies, but not to decide if they should go up and fight; they had already decided that. It was now a question of how?

We are in a new spiritual climate and we are no longer doubting if we can take on the giants. As an army rising in the earth, we are now waiting on the Lord to show us 'how' to fight. The church in prayer and practice is moving out against unrighteous rulers in the nations, those principalities and powers responsible for suffering, disease, death and destruction. God is calling His army to rise, declare and enforce His victory in our own lives, communities and in the nations.

e) Move forward, following the Ark of His Presence. (3:2-4)

> 'Three days later the Israelite officers went through the camp, giving these instructions to the people: "When you see the Levitical priests carrying the Ark of the Covenant of the Lord your God, move out from your positions and follow them. Since you have never traveled this way before, they will guide you. Stay about half a mile behind them, keeping a clear distance between you and the Ark. Make sure you don't come any closer."'

There is a time to cross out of the old and into the new. God will lead us, and His presence will go before us to bring us to a new dimension of possessing our inheritance. We as a people must know the voice of the Lord, hear His instructions and follow as His presence leads. We are a journeying people and this new era brings us to a new place in the spirit. We've not gone this way before. We have to go following His presence, there is no other way. To be successful in this, His presence must be the centrepiece, the whole focus so that we find our way through to the new place.

As a people of God, we must also ensure the proper protocol when dealing with the manifest presence of God. Our attitude must be one of honour, reverence and humility before the Lord's presence among us. As we move in the fullness of the seven-fold Spirit of God, we will understand and live in the Spirit of the 'fear of the Lord,' and delight in His presence among us.

We move forward to represent Him in the nations, so we honour that He is among us and goes before us.

f) Consecrate yourselves. (3:5)

'Then Joshua told the people, "Consecrate yourselves, for tomorrow the Lord will do great wonders among you"'.

In Hebrew, the word to 'consecrate' is hitpael, (hit·qad·dā·šū).

It means: to consecrate, sanctify, prepare, dedicate, be hallowed, be holy, be sanctified, be separate, to be set apart, be consecrated.

Just like the children of Israel, in this New Era, there is a call for the people of God to consecrate themselves. It is a call to be a people truly set apart for the purposes of God. God is calling us to examine ourselves and take time to allow God to incubate us into a people that are ready for His use.

At the beginning of 2020, the Lord said to me, 'It isn't business as usual.' That now appears to be an understatement. I believe we have an invitation to consecrate ourselves and set ourselves apart to rise in strength and be the people God has called us to be. We are called as a people set apart to display

His glory in the earth. It is a high and holy calling, and now, more than ever, let us come out of a 'normal' life and into an overcoming, abundant life.

We have the privilege of being chosen by God to be His ambassadors on the earth. He is calling us to set ourselves apart for Him. God is ready to display His goodness to the world. In the New Testament Paul declares, 'You are a royal priesthood, a Holy people, set apart to display the wonders of God'. God has given us opportunity to enter this new era, consecrated, separated and dedicated to a Holy life before Him. He is preparing a people to display His splendour!

I saw in the spirit a sieve. It was like one you would use in panning for gold. I saw that God was using it on us, His people. God is sifting out and disposing of the impurities. Over the past 12 months, I have seen the mesh of the sieve get finer and finer. Each time, it is sifting out more debris and refining His people in greater ways.

God is using this season of sifting and shaking to expose the impurities, but also to bring to the surface the treasures He has put in each one. He is going into the hidden places to bring light into darkness and cause things to be seen for what they really are. The pure will gleam with light and life while the impurity will be exposed so it can be discarded.

The unique giftings of each one of His people is being revealed, allowing each one to rise and shine in the place He has called us to.

God was about to use Joshua and the children of Israel to display His goodness and wonders across the earth. In the same way,

God is preparing a people in this New Era who have allowed Him to prepare them so that they may be used to do great signs and wonders across the earth that will bless all the peoples.

g) Remembering the Covenant Promises. (4:5-7)

> 'He told them, "Go into the middle of the Jordan, in front of the Ark of the Lord your God. Each of you must pick up one stone and carry it out on your shoulder— twelve stones in all, one for each of the twelve tribes of Israel. We will use these stones to build a memorial. In the future your children will ask you, 'What do these stones mean?' Then you can tell them, 'They remind us that the Jordan River stopped flowing when the Ark of the Lord's Covenant went across. These stones will stand as a memorial among the people of Israel forever.'"

The Ark was known as the 'Ark of His Presence' and also the 'Ark of the Covenant.'

We can only move forward as we move following the presence of God and keeping His covenant, front and centre.

Every time we take communion, we re-establish the covenant and remember all that Jesus did for us. Jesus himself encouraged us to, 'Do this to remember me'. (Luke 22:19)

We cannot keep covenant with God in our own strength. However, we now have a resurrected Saviour who has made a way for the covenant between God and man to remain unbroken. The power of communion enables us to live in unbroken fellowship with the Father, Son and Holy Spirit.

It is our privilege, by faith, to surrender to all that Jesus won for us in the new covenant. We now live with a new heart and a new mind and receive our covenant of sonship. We are the sons and daughters of the living God!

We take communion to also remember the victory of Jesus that enables us to receive our inheritance. We continue to remember the victory of Jesus among us and God's power available to us.

As we step into a new era it is important to remember that we are living in a new mindset and a new reality. We have crossed out of the old and into the new and now remind ourselves to live by the new mindsets that the Lord has brought us into. We cannot look back and pine for a more familiar time. Looking back only gives us opportunity to go back.

h) Circumcision of the Heart (5:2-3)

> 'At that time the Lord told Joshua, "Make flint knives and circumcise this second generation of Israelites." So Joshua made flint knives and circumcised the entire male population of Israel at Gibeath-haaraloth'.

We will be able to fully embrace this new era when we take the opportunity to rid ourselves of the flesh, and in New Testament terminology, circumcise our hearts again toward God.

Romans 2:29

> 'But you are Jewish because of the inward act of spiritual circumcision—a radical change that lays bare your heart'.

The shift into the new era is a necessary shift in our hearts. 'As we think in our heart, so are we.' Our hearts can be changed if we open them before God, softened and malleable in his hands. Hearts laid bare are soft hearts, open to change. In a new era of change, hearts must be softened again to receive from God the new things He is doing.

Hearts that will soften, forgive and love are always the key to finding God. Isaiah 6:10 tells us that hearts that turn, perceive and hear again, can be healed. God is looking for change again in His people. It will require soft hearts of repentance.

I hear God asking for surrender at this time. It is surrender to Him, surrender to the call of a softened, receptive heart that is ready to listen and do what God says to do. As we surrender with softened, repentant hearts, God will change us to become a people that will represent Him well on the earth.

We will become a people that can display His goodness and therefore His glory, so that the knowledge of the glory of the Lord can cover the earth like the waters cover the sea.

i) No more Shame (5:9)

> 'Then the Lord said to Joshua, "Today I have rolled away the shame of your slavery in Egypt." So that place has been called Gilgal to this day'.

God is supernaturally taking the shame of the old unfruitful season from His people. As we give ourselves to contend for a new identity as overcomers, I believe that the church of Jesus Christ will begin to be seen as the powerful force for life that she is.

In the New Testament, at the beginning of the church there were so many mighty miracles that were done among them, that it says the people were frightened.

I believe God is wanting to do this again. We will live in a Holy fear of God, because of His greatness and goodness being displayed through believers.

As we concentrate ourselves to the New Era, He will supernaturally roll off the shame. We are done with the old. As we refuse to bring the old mindsets and corrupted lifestyle into the New Era, His church will rise and shine with His glory.

In this new era, we consecrate ourselves to be used for the expansion of His Kingdom in the earth.

Like the Israelites, the church of Jesus Christ will not be known as a people wandering aimlessly in the desert, but they will be known as a forceful people who have authority to shift and change communities and nations.

Let the shame of the old season and the struggle of the wilderness season be stripped away and rise in the authority of Christ in you, the hope of glory!

Joshua 5:13-15 says,

'When Joshua was near the town of Jericho, he looked up and saw a man standing in front of him with sword in hand. Joshua went up to him and demanded, "Are you friend or foe?"

"Neither one," he replied. "I am the commander of the

Lord's army"'.

'At this, Joshua fell with his face to the ground in reverence. "I am at your command," Joshua said. "What do you want your servant to do?"

'The commander of the Lord's army replied, "Take off your sandals, for the place where you are standing is holy." And Joshua did as he was told'.

It is Jesus who is the commander-in-chief of the Lord's armies. He is the one who is in command. In this new era, we must understand that we are not looking to God, hoping He is on our side. We must surrender ourselves under His command and allow Him to lead us into the battle He has chosen for us.

We worship, pray and decree, as He leads us, using the weapons of our warfare to push back the enemy and establish God's Kingdom in the situation to which He has sent us.

Jesus himself is the Captain of the Hosts of Heaven's Armies and we are fighting with Him to advance the Kingdom of God on earth. As warriors in His army, He calls us to come alongside the 'Hosts of Angels' armies and receive instruction and direction from Jesus, our commander.

As Jesus strategically expands the Kingdom of Heaven on earth, we are privileged to fight and build under His command. In this New Era, God has prepared a generation to rise in the strength and power of God and bring answers to this world ravaged by sin. Jesus in His time on earth delivered multitudes from the power of the enemy. He also healed and restored and made whole. His army is called to do the same.

The earth is groaning under the weight of sin. It is groaning, quaking and shaking like it never has before. The weight of sin is causing chaos across the nations: famine, disease, floods, earthquakes, tsunamis and volcanic eruptions. The world doesn't have any answers, but Heaven does!

The Lord of the Host of Heaven's armies has divine strategies to ensure the Kingdom of God and the righteous rule of Heaven is established in the nations. God's army, God's people, are rising up to see the nations re-established under the authority of Heaven. I believe that we will see a move across the nations that will go beyond the impact of the Reformation of the 1700s. It is now time for the armies of God in the earth to join with the host of Heaven's Armies to shift and establish nations and people groups under the Lordship of Christ – because everyone wants a King like Jesus!

When God addressed Joshua and announced it was now time to take the promised land, Joshua made no excuses. Unlike the first time when the spies doubted their ability to take the land, this time there seemed to be no hesitation.

As Joshua stood up to lead the people, the situation had not really changed. There were still giants in the land and there were still major obstacles to be overcome. There were the Jordan River and the walls of Jericho, however there is no record that anyone was unwilling to go up and fight for their promised land and their inheritance. However, they had spent 40 years in the wilderness and the old generation had died. They would now rather fight than go back to living in the desert.

The church of Jesus Christ in this New Era seems poised in a similar position. No one wants to continue to live in the wilderness of doubt, unbelief, worldly ways and powerless Christianity any longer. There is now a generation ready to secure their identity, rise into their destiny and possess the promises that God has made available.

It is a leap of faith, just as was required by the first generation of Israelites. However, God in His kindness has brought His church to a place where we are ready to believe Him. I hear a 'roar' coming from the people of God who are declaring along with David, 'Who are these uncircumcised Philistines, that they should defy the armies of the living God'. [3]

CHAPTER FIVE

God's Authority in Bringing in a New Era

When God called Moses in the wilderness, He revealed Himself as the great I AM. This name of God had not before been revealed to anyone on earth. This revelation of the Lord Jehovah (Messiah Pre-Incarnate) as God, was necessary for Moses and for the children of Israel to hear and understand. Without it they would not have the faith and authority to stand against the power of Pharaoh over the land of Egypt.

God had determined to deliver the nation of Israel from their oppression. To enforce this promise, God had to reveal Himself in another dimension in the earth. Abraham, Isaac and Jacob knew God as God Almighty. He revealed Himself to them as God, the maker of heaven and earth. He revealed the knowledge that all belonged to Him and all could know Him as Elohim, God Almighty. God now reveals Himself to Moses, as the Lord, Jehovah, YHWH (Lord). [1]

God declared that He was the God that not only made the heavens and the earth, but the God that governs and rules the heavens and the earth. The God who is the Lord over all that is and has authority over all that exists.

God had purposed to reveal Himself as the great 'I Am that I Am',[2] not only to Israel, but to Egypt and the then known world. His ultimate authority as the Lord and ruler of the heavens and the earth was about to be displayed. He was using Israel, His chosen people, to do that.

God was displaying His sovereign power as 'I AM' (YHWH) when He delivered Israel from the bondage of the ruling powers of Egypt that were oppressing His people and keeping them in slavery.

God again displays His sovereign authority in the earth through the Lordship of Jesus. Jesus declared and proved that, 'Before Abraham was, I AM' (YHWH) [3] Jesus overcame to display Himself to the world as the supreme authority and power in the earth. Through His sinless life, death and resurrection, Jesus (I AM) revealed again His Lordship in the heavens, over the earth and under the earth. He displayed His authority to redeem all the earth back to Himself.

Moses received the new revelation of 'I AM' and used the authority of that name to completely destroy the ruling principalities and powers over Egypt. He then used this continuing revelation of who God is, to establish the people of Israel as a nation under divine law and order. Moses needed the revelation of I AM to shift the people of Israel from under the government of Pharaoh and into a new understanding of the government of God that they now lived under.

The revelation of Jesus, the I AM in all His facets is needed again in our generation to deliver His people, the body of Christ and the nations in the earth from the evil bondages of the ruling forces of the enemy over nations.

It is a vital necessity, as we press in to shift nations, to also know God, His character and His ways, in greater dimensions. As we receive greater revelation and have greater relationship with the Godhead, we can release by faith a greater dimension of His authority. When God's names are declared in all the many aspects of who He is, it releases greater dimensions of His authority, presence, and power on earth.

This great God, the great I AM, Jesus, has stepped onto the stage of history right now to enforce the covenant that He has made with His people, the body of Christ. The powerful arm of the Lord will be seen at this time across the earth. He is rising with His great authority and power through His people because of His commitment to keep His covenant.

This same God, the great I AM, is a covenant keeping God. He remembers His covenant and he keeps covenant with those who have made covenant with Him.

The New Era Of His Power

The rise and fall of kingdoms and nations is a hallmark of history. History is littered with the stories of the power play of nation rising against nation. Nations go to war against nations for many hundreds of reasons, yet as we have seen, it is God who rules the nations.

Psalms 2:6-9 says,

'For the Lord declares, "I have placed my chosen king on the throne in Jerusalem, on my holy mountain."

'The king proclaims the Lord's decree:

"'The Lord said to me, 'You are my son. Today I have become your Father.

'Only ask, and I will give you the nations as your inheritance, the whole earth as your possession.

'You will break them with an iron rod and smash them like clay pots. It is God who will have the last say and it will be His Kingdom that will eventually rule the earth'".

Jesus came to earth as a man and for the sake of humanity, conquered every power of the enemy in the heavens and on the earth. The promise that we can possess the land and establish the Kingdom of God for ourselves, our family, territory and nations, is sure.

As Lou Engle has said, 'God looks for someone who will step out of his or her insecurity and unbelief and rise up as a co-equal partner in the divine council of heaven to haggle with God—to make decisions with Him on what the future will be on earth, who demands in prayer on earth what God demands in heaven'. [4]

In the book of Daniel, we see Daniel interpreting a dream of King Nebuchadnezzar. This dream outlined an amazing dream of Kingdoms in the earth crumbling under 'a rock' cut from 'a mountain'.

Daniel 2:44-45

'During the reigns of those kings, the God of heaven will set up a kingdom that will never be destroyed or conquered. It will crush all these kingdoms into nothingness, and it will stand forever.

'That is the meaning of the rock cut from the mountain, though not by human hands, that crushed to pieces the statue of iron, bronze, clay, silver, and gold. The great God was showing the king what will happen in the future. The dream is true, and its meaning is certain'.

God gave Daniel the interpretation. The rock in this vision is the Kingdom of Christ Jesus which came into the world and overcame all the power of the enemy and bring this world back under the authority of the Kingdom of God. It is traditionally considered that the mixture of iron and clay in the King's dream, are the Roman and Greek empires that dominated the world in the time of Jesus birth and life here on earth. It was during this period that Jesus was born, died and rose again, overcoming all the powers in the earth, the heavens, and under the earth. It was at this time that the Kingdom of Heaven was hewed from the rock that is Christ and is continuing to advance forcefully in the earth.

The ancient Kingdoms of Rome and Greece dissolved, and the Kingdom of Christ is yet advancing across the earth. As Daniel's prophecy predicts, the Kingdom of God will overcome every other Kingdom in the earth. The Lord has promised His Kingdom is an everlasting Kingdom and the knowledge of His glory will cover the earth, as the waters cover the sea. [5]

In September 2014, I had a vision that confirmed what I suspected. God is calling forth a new band of warriors on assignment.

> *I saw this band of troops coming across the coastline. Their shields of gold were held high over their heads and locked together. The sun reflecting off these shields made the army look like a golden river flooding over the land. As they moved forward, they fanned out in separate tributaries, they ran like rivers across my nation of Australia. I knew that this was the army of God prepared, called, and was moving forward as one. They moved across the nation to make way to establish the Kingdom of God in the land.*

God is calling up His troops. He is calling not just an army, but a movement of His overcoming warriors to advance His Kingdom. It is for 'such a time as this!'

A new glory rests upon this people of God and the oneness between them is producing a movement that cannot be stopped.

God is raising up a movement of champion warriors across many nations. It is His army of over-comers, warriors of 'resurrection life', that will prepare the way for the great harvest that has been prophesied upon the earth. [6]

As the warriors of God move forward in overcoming prayer, with the shield of faith raised and locked together 'as one', the prayer of faith will release the power and presence of the Kingdom and reap hundreds and thousands of people across our nations.

Over recent years, each of these concepts discussed are shifting the focus of the body of Christ to impact all of society and transform communities, people groups and nations to live in the benefits of the Kingdom of God. God is calling His people to positions of influence to extend His Kingdom across all spheres of society in every nation. It is God's plan to see the Kingdoms of this world become the Kingdoms of our Lord and of His Christ.[7]

CHAPTER 6

A New Army for a New Era

An Army Mobilised By New Era Apostles And Prophets

Bishop Bill Hamon described in his book, *Apostles, Prophets and the Coming Move of God*, the systematic way in which God has rearranged the leadership of His church in the earth.[1] As discussed, the office of the apostle, prophet, evangelist, pastor, and teacher have now been established and given authority across much of the body of Christ.

We have seen apostles rise to give leadership to networks, groups of churches, apostolic hubs and apostle-led house churches. These groups cross the conventional lines of denominational groupings and instead gather around an apostolic leader.

God has given these apostolic leaders authority to gather those who look to them as apostolic fathers and mothers. We are seeing a return to the early church structure that recognises the leading and teaching of the apostles.

The establishing of this new, yet original government of God in the church on earth is perhaps the biggest and most impacting shift of the New Era. The government of God in the earth is established on the foundational teaching of the apostles and prophets and the five-fold offices in the body of Christ, Christ being the chief cornerstone. [2]

This directly impacts the effectiveness of the people of God as they rise as an army. The body of Christ, when effectively governed by the five-fold offices of the body of Christ, can advance forcefully. The five-fold offices facilitate and mobilise the army of God in the earth.

Apostles and apostolic hubs led by apostles and prophets are being established in the nations. Apostolic fathers of today understand the need to lead the body of Christ in the same way the apostles of the early church did.

Acts 6:4 says,
'They were given to prayer and the study of the word'.

These leaders understand the need for everything to come out of the place of relationship with the Holy Spirit, through prayer.

These new-look apostolic and prophetic leaders, who find themselves in the place of prayer, facilitate the release of prayer and the company of prayer warriors into their vital position in the Kingdom. This focus on prayer releases the prophetic word of direction for the apostolic hub. It gives clarity to 'hear what the spirit is saying to the church' so that the apostle can mobilize, at the spirit's leading, the church within their apostolic sphere of influence.

The apostolic leadership facilitates and supports the function of the prophetic prayer army, often gathered in houses of prayer, churches and homes. In turn, the prophetic prayer team-give direction and prayer support to the apostolic hub. The two function together to advance the Kingdom in regions and nations to which they are called. This company of prayer warriors 'make way for the King', opening the heavens and advancing the Kingdom of God in the sphere of influence for which they are responsible. This army crosses denominations, generations, and nations!

When the Apostolic Hub and the company of prayer warriors they have empowered are flowing together, the whole body moves forward at the unction and direction of the Lord. (3) The prophets and prayer company are understanding what the Spirit is saying to the 'church'. The apostles then facilitate the body of Christ moving forward with the knowledge of this direction.

This brings strength and equips the whole company belonging to that Hub. It releases the gifts and power of the Holy Spirit. The saints are equipped and released into their calling and destiny. The Kingdom of God is then extended, transforming families, communities, people groups and nations.

Apostolic hubs birthed in prayer, releasing the power of the Holy Spirit, equipping the saints to be released in all 7 mountains of society and fathering the next generation, can transform nations!

The army of God advances on its knees, and without the warriors in place, the Apostolic Hub is stalled in its endeavour to advance the Kingdom.

Aligned Under The Hosts Of Heaven's Armies

When God addressed Joshua and announced it was now time to take the promised land, Joshua made no excuses. Unlike the first time the spies doubted their ability to take the land, this time there seemed to be no hesitation.

As Joshua stood up to lead the people, the situation had not really changed. There were still giants in the land and there were still major obstacles to be overcome. There were the Jordan River and the walls of Jericho; however ,there is no record that anyone was unwilling to go up and fight for their promised land and their inheritance. However, they had spent 40 years in the wilderness and the old generation had died. They would now rather fight than go back to living in the desert!

The church of Jesus Christ in this New Era, seems poised in a similar position. No one wants to continue to live in the wilderness of doubt, unbelief, worldly ways and powerless Christianity any longer. There is now a generation ready to secure their identity, rise into their destiny and possess the promises that God has made available.

It is a leap of faith, just as was required by the first generation of Israelites. However, God in His kindness has brought His church to a place where we are ready to believe Him. I hear a 'roar' coming from the people of God who are declaring along with David, 'Who are these uncircumcised Philistines, that they should defy the armies of the living God?' [4]

Joshua 5:13-15 says,

'When Joshua was near the town of Jericho, he looked up and saw a man standing in front of him with sword in hand. Joshua went up to him and demanded, "Are you friend or foe?"

'"Neither one," he replied. "I am the commander of the Lord's army."

'At this, Joshua fell with his face to the ground in reverence. "I am at your command," Joshua said. "What do you want your servant to do?"

'The commander of the Lord's army replied, "Take off your sandals, for the place where you are standing is holy." And Joshua did as he was told'.

It is Jesus who is the commander-in-chief of the Lord's armies. He is the one who is in command. [5] In this New Era, we must understand that we are not looking to God hoping He is on our side. We must surrender ourselves under His command and allow Him to lead us into the battle He has chosen for us.

We worship, pray and decree as He leads us, using the weapons of our warfare to push back the enemy and establish God's Kingdom in the situation to which He has sent us.

Jesus himself is the Captain of the Hosts of Heaven's Armies and we are fighting with Him to advance the Kingdom of God on earth. As warriors in His army, He calls us to come alongside the Hosts of Angels' armies and receive instruction and direction from Jesus, our commander.

As Jesus strategically expands the Kingdom of Heaven on earth, we are privileged to fight and build under His command. In this New Era, God has prepared a generation to rise in strength and power to bring answers to this world ravaged by sin. Jesus, in His time on earth, delivered multitudes from the power of the enemy. He healed, restored and made people whole. His army is called to do the same.

The earth is groaning under the weight of sin. It is groaning, quaking and shaking like it never has before. The weight of sin is causing chaos across the nations: famine, disease, floods, earthquakes, tsunamis and volcanic eruptions. The world doesn't have any answers, but Heaven does!

The Lord of the Host of Heaven's armies has divine strategies to ensure the Kingdom of God and the righteous rule of Heaven is established in the nations. God's army, God's people, are rising up to see the nations re-established under the rulership of Heaven. I believe that we will see a move across the nations that will rival and go beyond the impact of The Reformation of the 1700s. It is now time for the armies of God in the earth, to join with the host of Heaven's Armies to shift and establish nations and people groups under the Lordship of Christ; because everyone wants a King like Jesus.

Equipped In The Place Of Prayer

To establish the Kingdom of Heaven on earth and see nations won for Christ, the army of the Lord on the earth must be called, trained, assigned and mobilized into the battle.

I heard the Lord say:

Ezekiel 37 is at hand!

I am calling up my warriors on the earth!

I am calling my troops to come into rank and file!

I am calling my people as a vast army, to rise into their full statue, for 'I have need of you in this hour.'

The kingdoms of this world are reeling and men's hearts are growing faint. It is time for my people to arise and extend my Kingdom to the sons and daughters of men devastated by the ravages of the enemy.

Rise in strength as the child of God that I have called and equipped you to be!

Rise in my overcoming, unrelenting, immovable fierce love that will motivate you to go beyond where you have gone before.

My fierce love requires a fierce commitment to gather the harvest of lost sons and daughters.

Rise in My power and the authority that I have released to you.

Roar, as a warrior of truth over the nations and fight for your sons and daughters, father and mothers, friends and family.

It will take a brave heart to move forward in courage across the nations and defy the enemy's plans.

It will take a surrendered heart, willing to lay down their life to bring in the harvest of lost peoples.

Rise as a lion in the nations.

Shine as a lamb among the peoples.

My Kingdom has come to the earth!

It is the clash of the kingdoms. Light versus darkness is becoming more intense across the earth. It is necessary that the army of God rise in who they are and whose they are.

God is training and mobilizing His new-look army that requires all the people of God.

1. Everyone a House of Prayer for the Nations

To advance the Kingdom of God throughout the nations, we must understand that we are all called to be part of the army. Each individual must have the mindset of a warrior, as we are all called to advance the Kingdom of God in our sphere of influence.

In Mark 11:17, Jesus displays His passion for the temple of God. He declares,

'My temple shall be a house of prayer for the nations.'

Later, in 1 Corinthians 3:16, Paul declares while addressing the assembly: 'You are the temple of the Holy Spirit.'

If we are the temple the Holy Spirit, then each one of us is a temple called a 'house of prayer for the nations'.

Just as Jesus cleansed the temple in Jerusalem, passionately declaring that it was to be a house of prayer for the nations, I believe that He is passionate now that His 'temple', each individual, be a house cleansed and full of prayer for the nations. Both individually and corporately, the Spirit of God is calling us as a house of prayer for the nations.

As we mature as sons and daughters of God and find ourselves friends of God, we will find that God's heart in us expands to cry out for Him that the nations be impacted with the love of the Father. Our own hearts also cry that Jesus receives His inheritance of the nations.

As each one recognizes we are a house of prayer and called collectively as a house of prayer, we will embrace the lifestyle of prayer and the need to be trained in the house of prayer as a prayer warrior. This is a role that everyone in the body of Christ must embrace.

2. The Example of Israel

In present day Israel, every man and woman who graduates from high school must spend time in military service. The women are enlisted for a mandatory 2 year period and the men for 3 years. After this time is up, most go on to embark on various other careers. However, some remain as soldiers, enlisted full time in the army. They go on to train in the many roles needed in an army. Other nations on the earth also adopt a similar practice.

The same must be true for the people of God. We may not all be full time specialists in the army, but we all need basic training so we are able to fight. We then have the skills to defend and occupy our own homes, communities, cities, and nations.

In Israel, if there is ever a crisis, every man and woman knows how to use their weapon and advance together as a troop. If the nation is ever under attack, all the home forces are called up. They have already been equipped and trained and are routinely re-trained. The defence force numbers can double or more, overnight. Indeed, everyone is Israel knows how to wield a weapon, is trained and ready when called upon.

This must also be true of the army of God. In times of crisis, individually or on a larger scale, we must all know how to rise up and fight. If we are trained, in times of crisis, when called as part of a community or national defence, we will show up and not hide. We can then make an important contribution to the army's effort.

The global CoVid-19 pandemic has highlighted the need for the whole army to be ready and willing to fight. It is necessary that every man and woman know their authority in Christ, be trained and can be called upon when the situation requires it. In fact, many houses of prayer and watchmen movements during this CoVid pandemic have joined together globally to push back this power of the enemy across the nations. With greater numbers comes greater power.

Matthew 18:19

'Again, I give you an eternal truth: If two of you agree to ask God for something in a symphony of prayer, my heavenly Father will do it for you'.

I believe this will become more and more important in this New Era. God has heard the cry of the oppressed and has risen to judge the principalities and powers over the nations to release justice into the earth.

I heard from heaven that the 'Gavel of God' has been released in the earth. God has risen to rescue His people and release a great harvest. The army of God on earth is pivotal to this forward thrust of the Kingdom across the earth.

3. Everyone Part of the Army

The idea that everyone in the body of Christ is part of the army is easily recognized when we believe that we are citizens of the Kingdom of Heaven on earth. As such, for the most part, we live and work in occupied territory.

In our personal lives and homes, we may attempt to live predominantly in God's Kingdom of righteousness, peace and joy. However, we may also be plagued by sickness, disease, poverty, strife, depression, relationship pain or any number of things perpetrated by the enemy. We are subject to evil forces, even though we live as righteous members of the Kingdom of God.

We also live in nations where the Kingdom of God is not the ruling mindset and culture of the nation. Our work and school life may not be governed by the principles of the Kingdom. All across nations and cultures, many other gods are worshiped, and ungodly rulers make unrighteous choices in the leadership of the territories, states and nations in which we live. These all influence our ability to reflect and advance the Kingdom in our sphere of influence. As such, we must be a resistance army.

A resistance army is a force that does all they can to resist the power of the enemy currently usurping the authority of the territory in which they live. Like Joshua, we must overcome the enemy in the territory that is promised to us and establish the rule of the Kingdom of God.

In WWII, Germany occupied France, and a French resistance army rose up. Everyone who was French who could be involved, was. Every man, woman and child did what they could to help protect their nation and restore their authority in the land.

At the same time in England, the country was under attack. Again, everybody became part of the army. Everyone did what they could. There were the land forces, the air force, the home guard, and the local war effort. All efforts were concentrated on winning the war. Everyone knew their assignment and position. In the battle of Dunkirk, everyday fishermen with their work boats, commercial vessels and even private yachts were all called as part of the effort to rescue soldiers from the coast of France. In a crisis, everyone becomes part of the army.

As the crisis subsided, roles changed. Some who started as the home guard went into full time service. Some recruits stayed as permanent troops in the army. Others went back into the work force and joined the home guard on the weekends.

Some stayed in the army so as to effect change in the nations they had defeated.

Whatever your position, everyone is vital to see the Kingdom of Heaven established on earth. As seasons and situations change, roles and responsibilities will change. However, it is vital that we understand our current role and position in the army. As a resistance army, we are all a part of the war effort in some dimension.

CHAPTER 7

Specialist Forces in the Kingdom Army

This army is facilitated, as we have seen, by apostles and prophets who are themselves 'given to prayer and the study of the word.'[(1)] The apostles and prophets as five-fold ministries take responsibility to equip and release the army of God.

This army will most often be trained and deployed from houses of prayer. God is raising up small groups, large groups, workplace groups, home groups and houses of prayer all across the body of Christ to train His army for this New Era. For ease of reference, I have called them Firehouses of Prayer.

These warriors are those who we may consider specialist forces in the army. As with any army, this army will be trained in the numerous types of warfare and roles to which they are called.

1. Types of Warfare in the House of Prayer

Warring Like Eagles

God is raising up specialist branches of His army. A spiritual Royal Air Force, a heavenly R.A.F. is being raised up to fight alongside the Hosts of Heaven's armies, to win the war in the air.

As any experienced military man will tell you, you must win the battle in the heavens before you can win it on the earth. These Firehouse warriors understand that they fight in the spiritual realm to conquer dark, unseen forces seeking to usurp the authority of the Kingdom of God on earth. [2]

As an army in the heavens, these R.A.F. prophetic warriors have been likened to an 'eagle army.'[3] An eagle army is an army of prophetic warriors, who perceive the spiritual realm. With accurate, heavenly insight, they use their weapons of warfare to defeat the enemy. They rise to pray, decree and establish Heaven's authority in a situation.

These warriors flow with the prophetic instructions of the Spirit, and in worship and prayer, use the weapons of warfare to overtake the power of the enemy. Knowing they are 'seated in heavenly places,' they fight from a position of authority, the position of an overcomer.

Knowing that Jesus has overcome all the power of the enemy gives this army confidence to enforce His will upon the earth. Following the lead of the Spirit, they can flow in prayer and sense that the Hosts of Heaven's Armies, the angel helpers have been deployed for the same assignment. [4]

The current prophetic word to the body of Christ is 'Rise and Shine'. This call is for NOW and it is no less significant or holy, than any other time in history. It is time for the armies of believers, who live from heaven to earth, to spread our wings and soar in the heavens.

It Is time to fly!

I heard the Lord say, *'It is a new way for a new day'*.

God is raising up His 'eagle' army. This troop of warriors sees from the heavens and fight from the authority of knowing that we are seated with Christ in heavenly realms far above principalities and powers. The 'eagle army' has been called to join forces with the Host of Heaven's Armies as they fight in the higher realms to release heaven to earth.

These eagle warriors bring the power and resource of heaven to earth.

The eagle warriors are prophetic warriors that 'see' well and 'see' from a distance what is happening in the earth realm. They see from the heavenly perspective and this makes them effective in their warfare on the earth. This eagle army is an 'air force' that wins the battles in the heavens so that the ground troops can advance in safety. This air force is a highly trained team of specialists in tactical manoeuvres that shift atmospheres over regions, so that the Kingdom advances in cities and nations.

Warring Like Ground Troops

The army of the Lord is also likened to soldiers on the battlefield. This is also a true and correct analogy. As soldiers, we fight the enemies of our soul and we bring down strongholds across the nations.

However, like Nehemiah, we are not just in a battle to push back the enemy. This is just the first step in establishing the Kingdom in the land where the enemy has been removed. We are in a battle not just to destroy the enemy but to establish the Kingdom of God. We are no longer content to only push back the enemy. As Jesus says in the gospels, if we make a clean sweep of the house and leave it bare, the enemy will come back in and possess the area that was cleared.[5] We must go on to establish the Kingdom.

The army of God needs to be aware of all the ways of God in battle. The Israelites were told many times to go and fight, but there were many other strategies used by the army of God. Waiting on God to hear His direction and strategy as Joshua did against Ai, as Deborah did with Barak, and as Elisha did with Ghazi, is essential to winning any battle. Again and again, scripture shows us that it is not by might and power but by the Spirit, that the battle is won.

Many times in the Old Testament we see the army of God ready for battle but never having to draw the sword, because God fought for them. We see the army go out to battle with the priests carrying the presence of the Lord and as they do, the enemy flees before the presence of the Lord. As with any divine assignment, we need 'Divine Intelligence'.

God works with His army in miraculous ways as they follow His strategy.

2. The Role of the Watchman Prophets in the House of Prayer:

At the rising up of the eagle armies, we recognized the necessity of the prophetic nature of this army.

In late 2017, a prophetic word was released by Charlie Shamp, a published prophet on the Elijah List, that encouraged the fact that there were more expressions of the prophetic across the body of Christ than had been identified at that time. We are beginning to discover the unique nature of each prophet and their specific call, giftings and metron, especially in the specialist forces.

Prophet Charlie Shamp released a prophetic word that defined three types of prophet. The third type of prophet that he mentions are the prophets that predominantly function in the house of prayer.[6]

Charlie Shamp's Prophetic Word

A New Prophetic Mantle of Three

The Lord spoke to me and said that He is stitching together a prophetic mantle, reserved in Heaven, for the new company of prophets He wants to release on the earth. He called them the Bridal company. This garment is being stitched together by a three-cord strand through the spirit of unity and bonded together through the bond of peace.

I heard the Lord say, "I am gathering from three different prophetic movements that I have birthed in the earth from the past. These were three distinct, heavenly birds that I sent to the earth, and they built prophetic nests for me. They have come home to Heaven, but they multiplied themselves and released their mantles upon their children before they left the earth.

"I will pull at their sons and daughters heart strings in this season with a new prophetic sound in an attempt to knit them together so their movements will fly as one. This will happen if they hear the new sound and catch the fresh wind that is about to come. When this happens, I will release a new prophetic movement—a new bird will come."

The Bridal Company—A Threefold Cord

I then saw in the spirit a mantle come out of Heaven carried by the wind of His Word. Engraved on this mantle was the phrase, "A threefold cord is not easily broken" (Ecclesiastes 4:12). Then I was shown the other side of the mantle. Engraved on this side were the words, "Behold, they are written in the book of Samuel the seer, and in the book of Nathan the prophet, and in the book of Gad the seer" (1 Chronicles 29:29).

I again heard the Lord say, "I am offering to the sons of the prophets the same mantle that I gave Elisha, a heavenly legacy. This is a double portion of the prophetic and is the inheritance only given to the first born, but I will lay it upon those who catch this new wind that I am releasing from My throne. They will receive it and fly together in the unity of the Spirit."

Suddenly, I saw a mighty, rushing wind released from the

throne room, and it blew across the earth. I saw three different birds take flight simultaneously and soar together as one.

The Golden Eagle

The golden eagle represented the seer prophets. Those who are given supernatural insights and heavenly revelation through dreams and visions. They carry a wonder-working power of the supernatural. They often manifest unusual wonders and manifestations of the glory.

The Silver Winged Dove

The silver winged dove represented the 'nabi' prophets. Those that spontaneously prophesy as the Spirit moves upon them. They are given a ministry of signs that manifest in the area of deliverance and healing.

The Snow White Owl

The snow white owl represented the prayer and holiness prophets. These are watchers and prophetic intercessors. They are those who the Lord had sent to pray and intercede over cities and nations. From out of this prophetic bird has sprung the prayer and purity revival movements.

As I looked at these three birds that took flight, I noticed each one had a face of a man. The golden eagle looked like a young prophet Bob Jones, his eyes piercing and laser-like, seeing directly into the heavens. The silver winged dove had the face of a young prophet Kenneth Hagin. His silver-tipped wings released healing and deliverance to the nations. The *snow-white owl had the face of a young Leonard Ravenhill. His eyes pierced the darkest of night and carried the wisdom of the heavenly Father.*

In this prophetic word, Charlie Shamp suggests there is another category of prophet, who represents the prayer and holiness movement. It is this prophet that is seen most clearly in prophetic intercession, watching in the place of prayer. These prophets for the most part have been hidden in houses of prayer. This New Era, however, necessitates that the role of the watchman-holiness-revival prophet be seen in order to advance God's purposes on earth.

Definition Of The Watchman Prophet

Charlie Shamp in his prophetic word makes reference to the scripture that differentiates types of prophets.

1 Chronicles 29:29

'Behold, they are written in the book of Samuel the seer, and in the book of Nathan the prophet, and in the book of Gad the seer'.

In this scripture, Nathan is referred to as a prophet. Here prophet is translated from the Hebrew word *nabi*. Nabi means 'to call - to announce.' This is the most common Old Testament term to designate a prophet. It is used over 300 times throughout scripture.[7]

Both Samuel and Gad are referred to as seer prophets and yet the Hebrew terminology is different: Samuel the seer

(Ro'eh); and Gad the seer (Chozeh). These two words translated as seer are two different Hebrew words. It would suggest that these two prophets operated in different ways although they were both known as seers. [8]

In his classic work *The Seer*, James Goll quotes the same passage from 1 Chronicles 29:29 that Charlie Shamp quotes. He uses it to distinguish different types of prophets and explains the difference between the two titles of 'seer' and 'prophet'. [9]

There is a reference in scripture showing the transition in terminology from seers to prophets. The two types of seer and the prophet were now collectively being referred to as prophets.

1 Samuel 9:9,

'(In those days if people wanted a message from God, they would say, "Let's go and ask the seer," for prophets used to be called seers)'.

So, we see in 1 Chronicles. 29:29; Samuel – Ro'eh; Nathan – Nabi'; and Gad – Chozeh; all three terms are used for the prophet's office. It would seem that the word prophet could now refer to many different expressions and gift mixes. [10]

Chuck Pierce in his book, *Re-Ordering your Day*, uses this same passage of 1 Chronicles 29:29, differentiating the seer and the prophet. Chuck makes the point that watchmen are called to watch and are therefore 'seers' as referred to in this passage. [11]

James Goll, in *The Seer*, makes this statement.'Not all

prophets are seers, but all seers are prophets.'[12]

It follows from these two statements that, if watchmen are seers, and all seers are prophets, then the watchman is a prophet. They are the same prophet that Charlie Shamp referred to in his prophetic word . They are the prayer, intercessor, watchmen, revival prophets, called as true prophets into the office of the Prophet.

As I waited on the Lord, I sensed a nudge: *Could it be that not all prophets are watchmen, but all watchmen are prophets'!*

Hosea 9:8 declares,

'The prophet is a watchman over Israel for my God'.

Ezekiel is the only prophet in scripture to be referred to and called by God as a watchman. Looking through Ezekiel's life gives us a fuller understanding of this third category of prophet, specifically called as a watchman.

1. Ezekiel – A Watchman Prophet

(i) Ezekiel was first called as a prophet.

Ezekiel 2:2-5

'"Stand up, son of man," said the voice. "I want to speak with you."

'The Spirit came into me as he spoke, and he set me on my feet. I listened carefully to his words. "Son of man," he said, "I am sending you to the nation of Israel…. and they will know that a prophet (nabi) has been in their midst"'.

Ezekiel, before he was known as a watchman, was known as a prophet.

Like Ezekiel, those who are watchmen will firstly be trained in the prophetic. The specialist watchmen in the House of Prayer out of necessity, operates in the gift of the prophet.

(ii) Ezekiel was then declared a watchman.

Ezekiel 3:16-17

'After seven days the Lord gave me a message. He said, "Son of man, I have appointed you as a watchman for Israel. Whenever you receive a message from me, warn people immediately"'.

After seven days, Ezekiel was called a watchman, to watch for Israel and to warn the people. He then became a watchman and prophet –hence, the unique call of a watchman prophet.

(iii) Ezekiel was specifically called to be a watchman prophet for Israel.

Ezekiel 33:7

'Now, son of man, I am making you a watchman for the people of Israel. Therefore, listen to what I say and warn them for me'.

As such, the watchman will have an affiliation and affection for natural Israel, its land and its people. They will have a heart to watch over the physical nation of Israel and pray for her.

Watchmen are passionate to see natural Israel fulfil her destiny. They know the pivotal role of Israel in advancing the Kingdom of God on earth.

The modern-day watchman will have a call also to watch over 'spiritual Israel', i.e. the church of Jesus Christ, who also are the people of God and the nation of God.

Watchmen are listening to hear, *'what the spirit is saying to the church.'* Their focus is to move the body of Christ into their position, ruling and reigning from heaven to earth across the nations. In this vital role, what the watchmen hear, they are responsible for releasing and often praying into being.

(iv) The watchman prophet is called to sound the alarm and give warnings.

Ezekiel 33:7

'I am making you a watchman for the people of Israel. Therefore. listen to what I say and warn the people for me'.

Watchmen are called to sound the alarm! There are significant repercussions for those who are called to this office and yet don't sound the alarm. It is a high and holy calling with great consequence and not a light thing to embrace. (Many have hesitated in identifying and embracing this call for this reason.)

Like Ezekiel, they understand that they speak for a righteous and just God. [13]

As such, the watchman is very aware of their call to a holy

and reverent lifestyle. The fear of the Lord is their delight! Indeed, it is a great delight to fear the Lord, for then you fear no other! [14]

(v) The watchman prophet has a focus on nations.

Throughout the book of Ezekiel, we see God give Ezekiel prophetic words firstly for Israel, then for the people and for the land. He also gives Ezekiel prophetic words for the nations surrounding Israel.[15] It seems the watchman prophet of today speaks into their own nation, into Israel and also into other nations.[16]

I heard the Lord say:

They speak not just to any peoples and situations, but they speak for Me to My people Israel, My land Israel and My nation Israel! both in the natural realm and the spiritual realm – the nation of the people of God scattered all over the earth! [17]

(vi) The watchman prophet knows their God.

They speak for a God of hope and restoration, calling the people of God into destiny spiritually and physically. The watchman has a passion to see the warriors arise and be the triumphant force in the earth that moves the Kingdom forward.[18]

(vii) The watchman prophet is aware of the heavenly realms.

Ezekiel 1:26-28

'Above this surface was something that looked like a throne made of blue lapis lazuli. And on this throne high above was a figure whose appearance resembled a man. From what appeared to be his waist up, he looked like gleaming amber, flickering like a fire. And from his waist down, he looked like a burning flame, shining with splendor. All around him was a glowing halo, like a rainbow shining in the clouds on a rainy day. This is what the glory of the Lord looked like to me. When I saw it, I fell face down on the ground, and I heard someone's voice speaking to me'.

We first meet Ezekiel as he explains his vision into the spiritual realm. Ezekiel had just had a vision of the glory of the Lord. At the close of the book of Ezekiel, we see him again explaining a heavenly dimension. A watchman prophet will be very aware of the heavenly realm and will spend time in the heavenly realms. Ezekiel saw the new Jerusalem. Watchman prophets will often see things a long way off. It again is often their role and joy to pray these things into being revealed upon the earth.

The Prophet And Watchman Prophet Working Together

As indicated in Charlie Shamp's word, there is evidence in scripture of how the prophet and the watchman prophet become a powerful team as they stood together. Here, Isaiah the prophet is speaking to the watchman and giving him a prophetic word of direction from the Lord.

Isaiah 21:6-10 (TPT)

'For this is what the Lord said to me:
"Go post a sentry and have him report what he sees.
When he sees them come with chariots
and advancing warriors riding on horses, donkeys, and
camels, let him be alert—extremely alert!"'

The Watchman obeys the word of the Lord to him through the prophet and stations himself at his watchtower. As he does this, he hears the word of the Lord.

Then the sentry cries out,

'I continually stand on this watchtower day after day
for you, O Lord.
I'm stationed at my post throughout the night.
Look! Someone's coming!
It's a man in a chariot with a team of horses.
He shouts out, 'Fallen, fallen, Babylon has fallen!
All the idols of their gods lie shattered on the ground!'"
My people, lying crushed on the threshing floor,
I declare to you what I have heard from the God of
Israel, Yahweh, the Commander of Angel Armies'.

The prophet and the watchman prophet are seen here in their specialist roles. As they work together, the word of the Lord for the nation is decreed.

As the different roles in the army are more defined, there is power in each playing their part. When two or more perceive a similar word and different expressions of that word are released, there is often the release of powerful decrees that make transactions in the spiritual realm. These have power to shift the atmosphere and situation being addressed.

This is the powerful result when the different prophetic expressions work together.

More Examples Of The Role Of The Watchman Prophet

We see other prophets in the scripture who also seem to fulfil various aspects of the role of the watchman.

Habakkuk

Habakkuk was another prophet who functioned as a watchman and had many characteristics of the watchman prophet. Habakkuk, as a prophet, although not specifically called a watchman, would appear to be the epitome of the watchman Prophet.

Habakkuk 2:1-3

'I will climb up to my watchtower, and stand at my guard post. There I will wait to see what the Lord says, and how he will answer my complaint. Then the Lord said to me,"Write my answer plainly on tablets, so that a runner can carry the correct message to others.

'This vision is for a future time. It describes the end, and it will be fulfilled. If it seems slow in coming, wait patiently, for it will surely take place. It will not be delayed"'.

It is thought that Habakkuk lived in Judah and was a contemporary of Jeremiah. Like Jeremiah, he probably lived to see the initial fulfilment of his prophecy when Jerusalem was attacked by the Babylonians in 597 BCE. Habakkuk watched over Judah, again suggesting that much of his role was as a watchman prophet.

Habakkuk had a watchtower from where he watched for what God was saying and doing over situations throughout the nation. He also refers to his watch tower as a guard post.

Being a watchman incorporates the sense that you are on guard. You watch over your sphere of responsibility to see that all is well, or to alert others if it is not.

Habakkuk hears from God and is told to write down the vision and make it plain, so that those who hear it can run with it.[19]

Those who are watchman prophets will relate very closely to this. God gets very specific with his timing, direction and information. So specific that if it is not written down, it can be forgotten.

The vision given to Habakkuk is not just for him, but for others to hear and understand. As the watchman, he is part of the army and is required to hear and see what the enemy is doing. It is then necessary for him to understand God's response and pass this information to the army to mobilize the response God has indicated.

Elijah

Elijah was a prophet who showed many characteristics of being a watchman.

1 Kings 18:38-40 says,

'Immediately the fire of the Lord flashed down from heaven and burned up the young bull, the wood, the stones, and the dust. It even licked up all the water in the trench!
'And when all the people saw it, they fell face down on the ground and cried out, "The Lord—he is God! Yes, the Lord is God!"
'Then Elijah commanded, "Seize all the prophets of Baal. Don't let a single one escape!" So the people seized them all, and Elijah took them down to the Kishon Valley and killed them there'.

Elijah watched over the nation of Israel (the Northern Kingdom). He was passionate to shift the nation back to worshipping God.

In recent times, God has been raising up prophets and watchmen with a focus to pray for and speak into nations. As the mandate of the body of Christ is to disciple nations, in this New Era, it will be important to raise up prophets with authority to speak into nations.

Elijah, with a display of the power and authority of God, turned a nation back to God and 'prepared the way of the Lord' in Israel.

John the Baptist, in the same spirit and power of Elijah, prepared the way of the Lord and shifted a nation in repentance, ready to receive Jesus.

God is raising up His prophets and prophetic warriors on the earth. There are emerging companies of watchmen and houses of prayer who, like Elijah, are called to prepare the way for the Lord across people groups and nations, for His Kingdom to come.

Daniel

Daniel was known as a statesman and a prophet, and yet he also fulfilled the role of a watchman in Babylon and for Israel. He is another example of a prophet with characteristics of a watchman in scripture. [20] Daniel, in particular, is a great example of the appointment, training and lifestyle of a watchman prophet.

i) He is called and appointed by the King. Daniel 1:4

'Select only strong, healthy, and good-looking young men....'

God does nothing by accident. God used the fact that Daniel was set in an extremely hostile situation. God has selected and appointed each one of His children to fulfil the role to which He has called them.

ii) The King takes responsibility to see that they are trained.

Daniel 1:3-4

Make sure they are well versed in every branch of learning, are gifted with knowledge and good judgment, and are suited to serve in the royal palace.

Daniel and his friends were trained in the ways of Babylon. Like Moses, He understood the world in which he lived so that he could skilfully address the authorities in the nation. A watchman has a keen understanding of what is happening in their assigned nations and can speak into this with understanding.

iii) Watchmen live with clean hands and a pure heart.

Daniel 1:8

'But Daniel was determined not to defile himself by eating the food and wine given to them by the king. He asked the chief of staff for permission not to eat these unacceptable foods.'

The watchman prophet has a passion for righteousness and holiness; they are often the champions of living a separated lifestyle, being in the world, but not of it.

(iv) Daniel was trained as a prophet.

He understood the spiritual realm and he knew God as the revealer of mysteries.

Daniel 2:22

'He reveals deep and mysterious things and knows what lies hidden in darkness, though he is surrounded by light.'

Daniel 1:17

'God gave these four young men an unusual aptitude for understanding every aspect of literature and wisdom. And God gave Daniel the special ability to interpret the meanings of visions and dreams.'

Daniel prayed and watched over Israel as well as Babylon, fulfilling one of the roles of the Watchman Prophet.

v) Daniel spoke into the king's personal life and His governing of the nation.

Daniel 4:19

'Upon hearing this, Daniel (also known as Belteshazzar) was overcome for a time, frightened by the meaning of the dream. Then the king said to him, 'Belteshazzar, don't be alarmed by the dream and what it means.'
'Belteshazzar replied, 'I wish the events foreshadowed in this dream would happen to your enemies, my lord, and not to you!'

Daniel spoke to the King of Babylon more than once, concerning the events of His Kingdom and nations.

(vi) Daniel had his own house of prayer.

Daniel 6:10

'But when Daniel learned that the law had been signed, he went home and knelt down as usual in his upstairs room, with its windows open toward Jerusalem. He prayed three times a day, just as he had always done, giving thanks to his God'.

Prayer was his regular habit, in which he watched for Jerusalem.

Daniel was unique in his call as is every prophet and watchman. However, the watchman prophet's call includes a call to the people of God, to the nations in which they live, to their unique sphere of influence and to Israel.

The Role of Watchman Prophets

Charlie Shamp continues his prophetic word.

Birthing the White Swan

These three birds caught the fresh wind of the Spirit, and as they flew together, this new mantle was placed around their shoulders. When this happened, they changed into a white swan and began to fly with grace and splendour.

I heard the Lord say: "This is My Bridal company! Those who have an ear to hear what the Spirit is saying to the Church. If you will fly together as one, a new prophetic movement will come. A new bird will be released—one the enemy can't stop nor hinder, one that carries grace, glory and splendour. This bird will rise to new heights, she will win every war, battle, and fight. Nothing will be withheld from My heavenly hands, for I've called My Bride to stand. The hosts of Heaven will be at her command! So unite and see My power come, for I've called My Bride to overcome!"

This fourth, heavenly bird represents the heavenly Bride that carries the spirit of the overcomer.

This heavenly bird is one that God wants the Church to give birth to in the earth, in this hour. It's a heavenly bird of grace, glory, and power!

I believe we are in a season of acceleration in the prophetic. A new mantle is being offered to the Church. God is looking for leaders to unite from these three movements. As they come together in this season, a new, fresh wave of prophetic power will be released upon this young prophetic generation of sons and daughters. It will take the spirit of Elijah coming upon the fathers and mothers to unite the different prophetic movements, but they will release a Bridal company, and a new prophetic bird will be released in the earth, one the world has never seen before. [21]

The watchman prophet is not new to the Kingdom of God, however in this New Era they are being revealed in the body of Christ as a vital part of extending the Kingdom of God in the earth. God is championing the watchman prophet in this New Era so:

1) This gift can be clearly understood and utilized by the body of Christ.
2) Those who have this gift and calling can understand, embrace and fulfil the destiny on their lives.

There are many whom God has trained prophetically and who are rising up as prophets in the house of prayer and watchman movement that we see emerging across the earth. They are those who have accepted a prophetic call on their lives, who have a passion to watch in prayer, and a growing heart for Israel, (spiritual and natural). Those who have been called to watch, God has gifted prophetically to fulfil this role.

3) The watchman prophet can be released to be heard as a prophet and;
4) He is then given the authority of the prophet to benefit and move the body of Christ forward in her authority to disciple nations.

Charlie Shamp's prophetic word indicates that there may be prophets leading these companies of prophetic watchmen and intercessors, who should be recognised in the Office of the Prophet to ensure the purposes of God can be outworked in the generation. It confirms the powerful effect of all the three prophetic streams working together.

Lou Engle, the leader of 'The Call' and now 'The Send', is the most obvious example of the watchman prophet in the world today. Lou has operated as a prayer leader in America and across the nations, calling thousands together in prayer, at the word of the Lord. His passion is to turn America back to God.

He is now identified among the council of the prophets in America. His recognition among the company of the prophets is a great step forward in advancing the Kingdom of God in this New Era.

Chuck Pierce says of the watchman:

'We need to recognise that watchmen are a critical part of the functioning of the body of Christ. We must set our watchmen into their positions.'[22]

A Company Of Watchman Prophets

Chuck Pierce, when speaking in Florida in December 2018, used the terminology 'Watchman Prophet'. He spoke that there was a new breed of leadership rising and He used Joshua as the example. [23] Joshua led a new army that made a way for a new era in Israel. God is doing the same today. He is raising up a new army to 'prepare the way of the Lord,' in this New Era. The new army in Israel was raised up to conquer the territories of nations and establish the people of God in their land of promise. God is raising up a new company today to conquer the spiritual enemies of nations and release them into Jesus' promise of life and life abundantly.

There is now a great release and mentoring needed of God's end time prayer army, down the generations and throughout the nations. God is raising up leaders who operate in the role of the watchman prophet to facilitate the eagle army, warriors of prayer, and the army that is the body of Christ to take territory.

Like the 'Company of Prophets', there is a 'Company of Watchman Prophets', who are trained together in houses of prayer, companies of prayers and prayer groups, under the leadership of apostles and prophets of prayer. These watchman prophets train together, and are held accountable and encouraged in their gift and call. They are equipped to move forward as an army to enforce the purposes of God in the earth.

Within the house of prayer, four main expressions of the prophetic watchmen have been currently identified. However, this is not exhaustive.

A company of:

1) Watchman Prophets

These prophets war with the prophetic direction and word of the Lord. They shift the heavens with the prophetic decree of the Lord.

They also take the role of leaders among the troop in prayer groups, prayer meetings and houses of prayer. They lead prophetically, hearing and decreeing what the Spirit is saying into the various situations they are called to.

2) Watchman Worshippers

The watchman worshippers war with their sound and movement.

There is an arising of the watchman worshipper, leading the army with the song of the Lord. Asaph was known as a prophet and we see him in the place of worship, leading worship before the Lord. [24] These worshippers have been assigned as psalmists, singing out the word of the Lord.

We see many examples in scripture where prophets led in worship and movement to win battles for Israel. Joshua's trumpeters went ahead of the battle.[25] Jehoshaphat's worshippers led the battle at Tekoa,[26] David worshipped and danced while bringing back the Arc of the Lord.⁽²⁷⁾ David's tabernacle was full of worship and movement and blessing to the people.⁽²⁸⁾

3) Watchman Priests

Anna, a prophet, ministered before the Lord both day and night, waiting for the revealing of the Messiah. There are many in the house of prayer whom God has set apart as those who minister before the Lord. It is a unique call and one that again is revealed in the place of prayer. Many prophets have as their first call a desire to minister in prayer and worship before the Lord.⁽²⁹⁾

4) Watchman Warriors with specialist roles.

This is the generic term for all who are part of the troop of prayer warriors in the army of the Lord. These are prophetic warriors that watch from the secret place and receive strategies from heaven. Under the leadership of the Lord of the Hosts of Heaven's armies, they wage war to take possession of what God has promised to His people: cities, generations and nations. They are the 'eagle army' that join with the hosts of heaven to win the war in the heavens, so that it can be won on the earth!

These watchman warriors are all are in various degrees of training. When training is completed, many will be specialists in different roles, as with any battle unit. The notable thing is that they prophetically pray, decree, move, mobilize and release the sounds of heaven into the earth to win spheres of influence for the Kingdom.

As such, the training of a watchman begins as the training of a prophet, for that is who the watchman is. Again, we use the example of Ezekiel 2:1 and 33:7.

In training, the watchman increases in levels of authority, understanding, gifts and anointing. They understand the metron to which they are called and the mandate to which we are called.

Jeremiah 1:7

'The Lord replied, "Don't say, 'I'm too young,' for you must go wherever I send you and say whatever I tell you"'.

Within the house of prayer, more and more specialist roles are being recognised as vital in moving the army forward to take new territory. There are many diverse watchman warriors rising together to prophesy in prayer, training together to enforce the Kingdom of God in the earth. These specialist warriors are becoming more specific in their roles. We see how effective this is in scripture.

2 Kings 11:4-15

Revolt against Athaliah

In the seventh year of Athaliah's reign, Jehoiada the priest summoned the commanders, the Carite mercenaries, and the palace guards to come to the Temple of the Lord. He made a solemn pact with them and made them swear an oath of loyalty there in the Lord's Temple; then he showed them the king's son.

Jehoiada told them, "This is what you must do. A third

of you who are on duty on the Sabbath are to guard the royal palace itself. Another third of you are to stand guard at the Sur Gate. And the final third must stand guard behind the palace guard. These three groups will all guard the palace. The other two units who are off duty on the Sabbath must stand guard for the king at the Lord's Temple. Form a bodyguard around the king and keep your weapons in hand. Kill anyone who tries to break through. Stay with the king wherever he goes."

So the commanders did everything as Jehoiada the priest ordered. The commanders took charge of the men reporting for duty that Sabbath, as well as those who were going off duty. They brought them all to Jehoiada the priest, and he supplied them with the spears and small shields that had once belonged to King David and were stored in the Temple of the Lord. The palace guards stationed themselves around the king, with their weapons ready. They formed a line from the south side of the Temple around to the north side and all around the altar.

Then Jehoiada brought out Joash, the king's son, placed the crown on his head, and presented him with a copy of God's laws. They anointed him and proclaimed him king, and everyone clapped their hands and shouted, "Long live the king!"

The Death of Athaliah

When Athaliah heard the noise made by the palace guards and the people, she hurried to the Lord's Temple to see what was happening. When she arrived, she saw the newly crowned king standing in his place of authority by the pillar, as was the custom at times of coronation. The commanders and trumpeters were surrounding him, and people from all over the land were rejoicing and blowing trumpets. When Athaliah saw all this, she tore her clothes in despair and shouted, "Treason! Treason!"

'Then Jehoiada the priest ordered the commanders who were in charge of the troops, "Take her to the soldiers in front of the Temple, and kill anyone who tries to rescue her." For the priest had said, "She must not be killed in the Temple of the Lord." So they seized her and led her out to the gate where horses enter the palace grounds, and she was killed there'.

This chapter is a picture of the priest/prophet working with the watchmen/guards and troops in the castle, to see God's governmental leader put into place.

The guards and troops of watchmen were who protected and ushered in King Josiah, as a boy King. At the same time, they ousted Queen Athaliah and killed the prophets of Baal and sacked the temple of Baal.

The guard/watchman, is clearly part of the army of troops

and works together with the army to enforce the prophetic word and victory for God's Kingdom.

As the different roles in the army are more defined, there is power in each playing their part. Often, when two discern the same thing, then the word of the Lord comes forth and the time to decree and what to decree becomes clear.

Much is accomplished in the spiritual realm when the power of the true word of the Lord is declared from the watchman prophet.

These watchmen, all across prayer groups and houses of prayer, are also now connecting throughout the earth for even greater impact in the nations.

They are becoming an army across the nations with a mandate to see nations shifted, discipled, and called into alignment with God's plan and purposes. They are an army that is releasing the prophetic word, song, dance and movement that shift atmospheres and enforce the government of God in the heavenly places and on the earth.

CHAPTER 8

The Lifestyle and Personal Profile of the Watchman

God's Perspective On The Watchman Prophet

The watchman prophet will relate to the following characteristics that God has outlined about the watchman prophet.

I heard the Lord say a watchman is:

-A vessel of My choosing and design.

-As a prophet, the watchman goes through a great refining process - tried and tested to come forth as gold. They are My beloved ones in the earth who speak for Me and hear My desire for the earth.

-As watchmen, they are doubly refined. The fire of purification is turned up seven times hotter. (This is a reference to Shadrach, Meshach, and Abednego being thrown into the fire.) ⁽¹⁾ *They speak not just to any peoples and situations, but they speak for Me to My people Israel, My land Israel and My nation Israel.* ⁽²⁾

Isaiah 62:6-7

'O Jerusalem, I have posted watchmen on your walls; they will pray day and night, continually. Take no rest, all you who pray to the Lord.
'Give the Lord no rest until he completes His work, until he makes Jerusalem the pride of the earth'.

The call of the watchmen today is also to speak to spiritual Israel, the church of Jesus Christ. The people of God, His church, scattered all over the earth, are needing watchmen who will watch and give warning of the advance of the enemy and how to combat his tactics and take ground for the people of God.

- The watchman prophet is, by nature, found in the secret place and often hidden where their voice is seldom heard by others. They are not seen very often in active leadership roles in the current church setting. In many cases they lead from behind through encouragement to devotion, holiness and zeal for the Lord to see His Kingdom being established on earth.

- Watchmen prophets are often hard to detect. They will be more comfortable in the secret place, in the back seat, in the prayer room, scribing what they hear the Lord saying, or worshipping before the Lord in the secret place.

In this New Era, God is calling them forth, not just for prominence or promotion, but to be identified and established as the necessary and vital part of the army of the Lord as He moves His Kingdom into dominance in the earth.

In these times of war, the watchmen trained as prophets, worshippers, warriors, and priests are necessary in the battle. We must champion their voice to be heard as they watch in these critical times. They are necessary in the battle for new lands, territories, and spheres of influence to be secured under the rule of Jesus.

The Ancient Path And The Peculiar Call Of The Watchman

The watchman makes a vital and valuable contribution to the advancing of the army of the Lord in their quest to take possession of new territory.

1. **They will lead from and remain in the secret place.**

   Anna the prophetess of the New Testament is an amazing example of the watchman prophet who watched and waited on the Lord in the temple day and night. Her prayer and fasting watched over Jesus being born into the earth.

Luke 2:36-38

'Anna, a prophet, was also there in the Temple. She was the daughter of Phanuel from the tribe of Asher, and she was very old. Her husband died when they had been married only seven years. Then she lived as a widow to the age of eighty-four. She never left the Temple but stayed there day and night, worshiping God with fasting and prayer. She came along just as Simeon was talking with Mary and Joseph, and she began praising God. She talked about the child to everyone who had been waiting expectantly for God to rescue Jerusalem'.

2. **They will not move out without a clear word.**

Deborah, a prophetess of the Old Testament is a great example.

Judges 4:6-7

'She said to him, "This is what the Lord, the God of Israel, commands you: Call out 10,000 warriors from the tribes of Naphtali and Zebulun at Mount Tabor. And I will call out Sisera, commander of Jabin's army, along with his chariots and warriors, to the Kishon River. There I will give you victory over him."'

3. **They are clear in their mission and the Word is strong in their mouth.**

Proverbs 16:10-13 (TPT)

'A king speaks the revelation of truth,

so he must be extraordinarily careful in the decrees that he makes.

The Lord expects you to be fair in every business deal,

for he is the one who sets the standards for righteousness.

Kings and leaders despise wrongdoing,

for the true authority to rule and reign

is built on a foundation of righteousness.

Kings and leaders love to hear godly counsel,

and they love those who tell them the truth'.

4. **Their commitment to purity and holiness keeps them focused on the narrow way.**

Psalms 24:7-9

'So wake up, you living gateways!

Lift up your heads, you ageless doors of destiny!

Welcome the King of Glory,

for he is about to come through you.

You ask, "Who is this Glory-King?"

The Lord, armed and ready for battle,

the Mighty One, invincible in every way!

So wake up, you living gateways, and rejoice!

Fling wide, you ageless doors of destiny!

Here he comes; the King of Glory is ready to come in!'

Personal Profile Of A Prophet, Priest, Worshipper And Warrior Watchman

As the watchman prophet has emerged, there has been a greater understanding of the various aptitudes and attitudes that they carry.

Purpose Of The Call

Psalm 16,17

It is a necessary part of the role of the watchman to live as a friend of God. Without this friendship, the watchman cannot fulfil the role to which he is called.

Jesus' statement in John 15:15 'Without me, you can do nothing' is a truth that is necessary for every watchman to embrace.

Psalms 16:11

'For you bring me a continual revelation of resurrection, the path to the bliss that brings me face-to-face with you'.

Psalms 17:2

'Lord, I always live my life before your face'.

Like Jesus, the watchman's purpose is *'to glorify the Father on the earth'*. In oneness with Jesus and each other, they call heaven to earth to give Jesus the glory due His name.

John 17:1

'Father, the time has come, unveil the glorious splendour of your Son, so that I will magnify your glory!'

Parameters

Genesis 16,17

Genesis 16 and 17 tell the story of the birth of Ishmael and the devastating effect this had on the purposes of God upon the earth. It seems that Ishmael was born from Abraham and Sarah's desire and not in God's timing.

My husband Bruce often says, 'God's will at the wrong time is a disaster!'

Genesis 16:15-16

'So Hagar gave Abram a son, and Abram named him Ishmael. Abram was eighty-six years old when Ishmael was born'.

Ishmael was born the son of Abram. However, Isaac was born the son of Abraham. Between the time Ishmael was born and the time that Isaac was born, God encountered Abram and changed His name to Abraham. God changed Abram's name and with it his identity. God established a greater dimension of faith and character in Abraham that prepared him to father a nation.

God is doing a great work in all our lives to prepare us to

bring His will and blessing into the earth. He is shifting and changing and establishing our identities to more fully reflect who He is on the earth. The fullness of God's blessing will be seen on the earth when we follow Him in His timing. Like Abraham, we will not release all that God has for us if we do it outside of His divine time.

The timing of God is crucial in the life of a watchman. Throughout scripture, God is very specific about dates and times, and Solomon declares there is a time for everything. [3] God is intentional about His will being accomplished at specific times. Having the right time for an incident or event is crucial to the advancing of God's Kingdom on earth. Jesus was a prime example.[4] The New Era in which we find ourselves, is a 'kairos' time in God's calendar, and He is preparing His people, for He has chosen now to do mighty things in the earth!

God requires His people to live by His times. He was specific about when the Israelites celebrated the feasts, for they were prophetic pictures of what God would accomplish through Jesus. [5]

God was specific about days and times to go to battle. We see it throughout the Old Testament. Joshua, Gideon, Samson and many others were given specific times for the battles they fought. [6] We see this when Elijah called Ahab and the prophets of Baal to Mt. Carmel. He repaired the altar and offered the sacrifice at the time of the afternoon sacrifice.

The times of the sacrifices were all outlined in the Torah for the people to follow. [7]

As such, a watchman who watches over and for the people must be very aware of the times and seasons, spaces and places in which they watch. In the Old Testament times, each day was divided into watches set by the rising and setting of the sun. In later centuries, the watchman were seen at the city gates as the town criers, watching what 'time' it was in the city and what was happening in the city. In fact, that is why your watch today is called a watch! The watchman, by virtue of what He did, set the time. Watchmen are responsible to call forth the time and seasons at the Lord's unction.

As watchmen, part of the job is to be alert to watch for the new day approaching and to declare it forth at the right time! Understanding the times and seasons of God and the timing He has for events in the earth is vital to advance the people of God in God's time to accomplish the advancing of the Kingdom in the earth and across the nations.

Provision

Exodus 16, 17

The old saying, 'Where God guides, He provides' remains true. God provides for us as a loving Father and we can have faith in His provision for all our needs. God's wonderful provision for His children is seen markedly in the people's call out of Egypt and the necessary wilderness crossing.

Exodus 16:4-5

'Then the Lord said to Moses, "Look, I'm going to rain down food from heaven for you. Each day the people can go out and pick up as much food as they need for that day. I will test them in this to see whether or not they will follow my instructions. On the sixth day they will gather food, and when they prepare it, there will be twice as much as usual"'.

When God has specifically led us into an assignment to advance His Kingdom, we can be sure of His provision. At God's leadership and direction, we can be confident of His provision. God led the children of Israel out of Egypt to the Red Sea. It was a strange but crucial move for the Israelites. Without this step, the Egyptians would have overtaken them in the desert and returned them to Egypt. Both the leading to the Red Sea and the provision of the way through it was God's divine providence. We can trust a loving heavenly Father to lead us to the places that are necessary for us to go and provide for us all the way. We must trust His heart of love for us, His children. It was the same as they made their way across the desert. God gave manna in the desert and water from the rock.

The watchman lives in faith that what God has assigned, he will provide for. Every prayer assignment prophetically fashioned will have God's provision. The Father has supernatural provision for the assignment on every level. When the Host of Heaven's armies releases an assignment, He will provide supernatural provision of more than enough.

Peace

Genesis 33

When it was time for Jacob (Israel) to be re-established in the land of His inheritance, God supernaturally established him in peace.

Jacob's life had been peppered with rivalry. He firstly had contention with his brother and then also with his uncle Laban when he moved to establish his own family. He even had contention in his own household between his wives.

However, when Jacob obeys God's leading to return home to the land of his inheritance, God honours him by ensuring that he returns home in peace.

God supernaturally gave Laban a dream so that Laban would allow Jacob to leave peacefully.

Jacob and his whole family were then re-united with Easu in peace. This was a miracle. Only God could have brought this peace.

In this New Era, it is time for the people of God to receive their inheritance, it is time to rise up and take the 'land' God has promised and establish His Kingdom.

Look to God to establish right relationships and peace with those around you. Living in peace will establish you in your inheritance and will establish nations to fully possess their inheritance.

Presence

Exodus 33

'Then Moses said, "If you don't personally go with us, don't make us leave this place. How will anyone know that you look favorably on me—on me and on your people—if you don't go with us? For your presence among us sets your people and me apart from all other people on the earth"'.

God's manifest presence with us will distinguish us as a people set apart for God. When the presence of God surrounds our atmosphere and worship is our routine, God's guiding presence will be among us.

It is time for the people of God to again be distinguished in the earth by His presence and authority among us.

Jesus baffled the scholars and the people because when He spoke, He had authority unlike the teachers they were used to. Peter also confounded the scholars because He spoke with clarity and the testimony was that he had been with Jesus.

When the presence of God empowers us in the secret place to pray His will, then we know our prayer is effective in the heavens and on the earth. Through our decrees we can speak God's will into the earth!

Praise

Psalm 33

Praise and worship must be central to who we are and what we establish in the Kingdom. Heaven has at its centre the throne surrounded with constant worship.

To establish heaven on earth, it will be necessary to establish worship in our midst. This will need to be our personal practice and also our corporate practice. It will be necessary for families, cities, and nations.

When David ruled in Israel, He established the tabernacle of David, in which he organized 24/7 worship. With worship established in the midst of the nation, the nation flourished, and Israel was established and secured as a nation. By the time Solomon came to the throne, Israel 'had peace on all sides'.

Releasing worship in the earth is vital to the establishing of the Kingdom, personally, corporately and for the nations.

Ruth Heflin wrote in her book, *Glory*, that in her house of prayer, they would sing until the presence came and worship until the glory came. God encouraged her saying, 'Everything you need is in the glory!' [8]

When we find Him in His glory and release to Him the worship due His name, everything we need will be released to us to extend His Kingdom.

As we receive from Him, we then release back the praise and glory due His name. 'For from Him and through Him and to Him are all things, to God be the glory forever, Amen!'

God gets all the glory, thanks and praise!

Promises

Jeremiah 33:3

It is the privilege of the watchman to watch, hear and understand from the Spirit things that we do not know in the natural. It is this understanding that propels us forward to be effective in our prayers and effective in establishing righteousness in the land so that blessing and fruitfulness can flow.

Jeremiah 33:3

'Ask me and I will tell you remarkable secrets you do not know about things to come'.

As we follow the leading of the Spirit, the Spirit delights to reveal the mysteries of God and superior wisdom to ensure victory over all the power of the enemy.

These strategic revelations will enable the warriors to be at the right place at the right time. With strategic keys, just as individuals can be shifted and released, so can nations and land be freed from an unrighteous past. Trauma can be broken off the land and righteousness and peace loosed to restore the land.

David enquired of the Lord why there was famine in the land. The Lord gave him a clear answer and when repented of and rectified, the famine was halted in the land and the people were again able to flourish. In the Old Testament, the price of sin was paid for by the people. In this New Testament generation, we have access to the blood of Jesus, that has paid the price, fulfilling all righteousness to restore the land and the people. [9]

Passion

Ezekiel 3:16-17

In this passage, God addresses Ezekiel as a watchman with the mandate to warn the people about what he sees and hears.

'Son of man, I have appointed you as a watchman for Israel. Whenever you receive a message from me, warn people immediately'.

God impassions His watchmen with the knowledge that to obey the Lord is more essential than fearing what man might do. Jeremiah was given the same instruction. He was to obey and not compromise His call. [10]

This passion is fuelled by the spirit of the fear of the Lord and scripture announces that in this, there is great delight. [11]

In an encounter with the Lord, I saw myself suddenly clothed in a turtleneck-type sweater that reached down to my knees. I knew it was the spirit of the fear of the Lord. I had a great sense of every part of me being held in divine order and peace. There was a deep awareness of the presence of God and His comfort in it. Indeed, it was a great delight as I realised that while wearing this sweater I had absolutely no fear of anything. I was totally free, and joy and delight invaded me.

I believe the spirit of the fear of the Lord will empower and impassion His warriors to be bold in this New Era to 'speak the word of the Lord' as the Lord releases it.

Watchmen In The House Of Prayer - Firehouses

Watchman Warriors are mostly found in prayer communities, prayer groups and houses of prayer. We call these houses of prayers 'Firehouses' as they burn passionately with the fire of love, the fire of purity and the fire of zeal.

These Firehouses give permission to all, no matter what sector or rank of the army they are currently in, to pray. Having a prayer meeting only requires one other like-minded, like-hearted, wholly devoted person who will agree and meet to pray. You do not need to wait for your church to call a prayer meeting. You do not have to wait for a Zoom prayer meeting call. You are a house of prayer and you only need a passion to pray and one other person to agree with you.

The Firehouses release those who pray and have a passion for prayer to be an effective part of the force of prayer, extending the Kingdom. Prayer is no longer something done when there is a need, when the church calls a prayer meeting or when someone asks you to pray. Prayer is a lifestyle that every christian partakes in, because we are people who live in a vital relationship with God the Father, the Son and Holy Spirit.

Our relationship with God develops through prayer. Prayer is communication with the Godhead. Those who come into a closer and closer relationship with the Lord will hear and obey His voice. From this place of prayer, the Lord leads and teaches and prepares His people as houses of prayer for the nations.

The Firehouses are small and large gatherings in homes, churches, businesses, and schools across communities that facilitate prayer to see the Kingdom come. God is raising up Firehouses to cover every sector of society across nations with an aim to see 'on earth as it is in heaven.'

The Firehouses are places where each one knows they are 'a house of prayer for the nations' and can join together to truly see 'shift' in the nations.

Firehouses Of Prayer Are Empowered By The Holy Spirit's Baptism With Fire.

The fire of the Holy Spirit releases the fire of passionate love, power, and light to enable and equip the prayer warrior to see from a heavenly perspective and release the necessary weapons to overpower the enemy.

Love is a passionate fire, extended from the Father to bring salvation to all people. This love motivates and empowers the warriors to continue in the fight for the nations. Firehouses meet in homes, community centres, local schools, and churches, to fuel the power of prayer all across communities, cities and nations.

The fire of the Holy Spirit, like any fire, releases power and fire into anything that it comes into contact with. It emboldens and empowers whatever is ignited by it. This fire has a power to shift and change every circumstance to which it is introduced. The force of the fire can become unusually powerful as others catch its flame, or it can be contained to enable and provide for the sustaining of life.

This fire has within it a cleansing ability. It will purify the heart of those who embrace it. 'The pure in heart will see God.' [12] To embrace the purifying work of the Holy Spirit is a joy, for it enables us to see God more clearly and fulfils the deep longing of our heart to know the Father closely and intimately. To see the Father is to 'know' Him in greater ways and greater measure.

This fire is necessary to bring the Bride into her position as a Bride without spot or wrinkle. A Bride fit for her bridegroom. As a warrior bride, the aim is to be like Jesus and reflect and represent Him on earth. No firehouse can function without the empowering of the Holy Spirit fire.

This Holy Spirit fire is the light of God that gives direction and understanding necessary for the Watchman. It is a light in the darkness and releases the light of life, joy and peace into the House of prayer. This joy strengthens, encourages, and revives His warriors. This passionate joy celebrates the victories that the Lord brings and releases more joy and life into the House of prayer.

Isaiah 56:7 tells us there will be joy in the house of prayer!

In any Firehouse of prayer, it is vital to stop and celebrate the victories and rejoice with heaven, for heaven rejoices over battles won!

The power of the Holy Spirit in and through His people is the same resurrection power that raised Jesus from the dead. As such, there should be abundant life spilling from the house of prayer.

No warrior can be successful if they are never rested. Some situations will call for a long and intense campaign; however, be aware of your limits and allow the Lord to give you rest.

Whole, Holy And Wholly Devoted

For those who would be specialists in His army, they are called especially to be Holy, Whole and Wholly Devoted!

Holy

To be Holy is to be separated out to be used in the service of God. In Old Testament times, the articles of the temple were considered Holy, because they were used exclusively in serving God. He had specifically given instruction on how, when and where they were to be used.

God has called His body 'a holy people set apart to Him'. Firehouses are set apart as holy to stand in the righteous ways of God, not having any tolerance for the things of the world, the flesh and the devil. This gives authority in the heavens and the earth.

Holiness is a separation from the common things of life into a life full of heaven's abundance; to partner with the armies of Heaven, under the Lordship of Jesus Christ in a high and holy calling. You are not your own, you are bought with a price. You are a chosen generation, a royal priesthood, a holy nation.[13]

People identified and proclaimed as a people of God and part of the Army of the Lord must be separated, different, and a peculiar people, distinguishable from every other nation. Not because of their dress, hairstyles or quirky characteristics, but because of the love, life and power of God manifested through them.

It is indeed a high and holy calling. It takes people out of the mundane and ordinary into a realm of living that brings abundant life and overcoming strength.

Whole

God in His kindness trains us as part of His army. Army training begins with training in personal discipline. Any army will first train their troops in discipline. As troops we learn to have authority over our own lives. As prayer warriors and members of Christ's army, the Lord will teach us self-disciple and how to use our weapons effectively in our own situation first. We learn to defeat the enemy in our own territory and have authority in the situations in our own lives.

As we gain authority in our own lives, then we have authority to train and agree with others in broader realms of influence. Later you may specialise in the area to which they are called. Each time you take ground, you have authority, ability and capability to lead others to overcome in those realms.

Some are trained in many different areas, so they gain experience and authority to then teach, train and lead others in the battles that God assigns them.

Our training must include training in righteousness and wholeness. Jesus said, 'The enemy is here, but he has nothing in me'.[14] Jesus resisted to the point of sweating blood but He never sinned. The enemy had nothing in Him that he could use to overcome Him.

There was absolutely nothing in Jesus that agreed with the enemy. As such the enemy had no legal right to enter his domain of authority.

Authority in life comes through the resurrection power of Jesus. We are to enforce this rulership of Jesus wherever we go. Our own righteous stand will mean that the enemy has no authority to take our victories from us.

Your victories will ultimately transfer into victories for your family, your city, the nation and the nations.

Wholly Devoted

A life with whole-hearted devotion to a loving God calls us into destiny. It is a life in which we live in realms beyond our own possibilities. This is a life where we are privileged to see more and more of the Kingdom open to us. This Kingdom will flow through us as we lay down our own will and ways.

In this New Era of Glory, the glory realms of the spirit are opening in revelation to us like we have not seen in our generation. As we enter this 'New Era of glory', the battle strategies are changing. In modern warfare, the battle has changed and the weapons are more advanced. The same is true with the Firehouses of prayer.

In this New Era, God has promised 'remarkable miracles and spectacular victories.'

Being part of His army is being invited to embrace and see the victories that a loving, heavenly Father is pleased to give His children. It is being part of a team that calls His Kingdom into the earth.

Part 2
Shift the Nations

CHAPTER 9

God's Strategy for the Nations

It Is Time To Shift The Nations!

In order to bring His Lordship and the government of God to rule and reign in the earth, God is targeting a shift and change across the nations.

I believe that God is targeting the 'discipling' of the nations, as commanded in Matthew 28:19-20:

'Then Jesus came close to them and said, "All the authority of the universe has been given to me.

Now go in my authority and make disciples of all nations, baptizing them in the name of the Father, the Son, and the Holy Spirit.

And teach them to faithfully follow all that I have commanded you. And never forget that I am with you every day, even to the completion of this age.'"

God has always used nations and people groups to enforce His will in the earth.

God called Abraham and made him into a nation.

He used the nation of Israel to be a prototype of a nation governed by God. He then gave Israel the privilege of bringing forth a Son, Yeshua, to rule as a King over the nation and the nations.

Genesis 18:18-19 says,

'For Abraham will certainly become a great and mighty nation, and all the nations of the earth will be blessed through him.

'I have singled him out so that he will direct his sons and their families to keep the way of the Lord by doing what is right and just. Then I will do for Abraham all that I have promised'.

Through Jesus, God established another nation. God calls His people on earth a nation.

As 1 Peter 2:9 says,

'But you are God's chosen treasure—priests who are kings, a spiritual nation set apart as God's devoted ones. He called you out of darkness to experience his marvellous light, and now he claims you as his very own. He did this so that you would broadcast his glorious wonders throughout the world'.

Through the nation that is the body of Christ, the Lord is moving out across the earth's nations to establish His Kingdom. One of the ways this is expressed is through His righteous rule and reign across the nations of the earth.

When Jesus ascended to heaven, He instructed — in fact, He commanded — His disciples to 'Go and make disciples of the nations' [1]

Matthew Henry in His commentary on this verse asks and answers this question:

'What is the principal intention of this commission? The answer is to disciple all nations'

Henry explains that the original Greek word used in Matthew 28:19 for disciple was *'mathetusate.'* [2]

He explains this word *matheteusate* means to 'admit them as disciples; do your utmost to make the nations Christian nations'.

Therefore *'go, and disciple them'*.

He then clarifies … 'the achievements of the mighty heroes of the world were nothing to it. They conquered the nations for themselves and made them miserable; the apostles conquered them for Christ, and made them happy'. [3]

Jesus asked that we pray, 'His Kingdom come, His will be done, on earth as it is in heaven.' [4]

As such, the discipling of nations makes a way for the

advancing of His Kingdom and the answer to this prayer. This is the fulfilment of God's plan which He expressed to Abraham when He said, 'Through you, all the nations of the earth will be blessed'. [5]

We, as a people of God, have the privilege of making way for the King of Glory to continue to advance His Kingdom in the earth and bless the people and the nations.

In His kindness He tells us of His plans, 'The Lord does nothing unless He first tells his prophets'! [6] If we hear His voice and join with the prayers of heaven, then mercy can flow, and a wall of righteousness can be established to guard the nations and the land.

Nations can be discipled as the people of God rise to embrace their call as an army of prayer warriors for the nations.

Jeremiah 51:20 (NKJV) says,

'You are my battleaxe and weapons of war.'

The word of the Lord, in the mouth of His people who speak with His authority, has power to rescue and establish nations and bring them under the Lordship of Christ.

We see that Abraham stood in the gap for Sodom and Gomorrah, but righteousness was not found in the city and it was unfortunately destroyed. [7] Jonah prayed for Nineveh, and they repented and righteous judgement was averted. [8]

It was Elijah who confronted ungodly leadership in Israel and prepared a way for the nation of Israel to turn back to

God. Elijah displayed the power of God, calling down fire from Heaven. He also displayed the authority of God, taking off the heads of those in authority who stood against God. (9) In Elijah's time, heads literally rolled.

In today's world, I believe that spiritual heads ruling the unseen realm must be deposed, and corrupt leadership exposed.

When Elijah dealt with the prophets of Baal, this ultimately led to a change of leadership in Israel and Godly kings being re-established in the nation.

In the same spirit of Elijah, I believe that the Lord in this New Era is raising up an army greater than we have ever seen in the body of Christ.

This army of champions is being raised up 'to prepare the way of the Lord!' in the same spirit of Elijah and John the Baptist, who were both called to 'prepare the way for the Lord'.(10)

These Godly prayer warriors will advance His Kingdom, enthroning Jesus over nations and making a way for God's choice of leadership to be established across nations in this New Era of glory and harvest!

Isaiah declared, 'Prepare the way of the Lord, make straight paths for him.' (11) John the Baptist echoed this sentiment declaring that it was his job to 'make way for the Lord's coming.' (12)

He did this by calling the people to repentance and turning

their hearts to God.

Jesus tells us in Matthew 17:12 that John the Baptist operated in the same spirit that Elijah had.

Elijah turned the nation of Israel back to God by confronting ungodly mindsets, displaying the power of God and calling the people back to God.

There is an army that is rising with the same mandate, to confront ungodly mindsets, display the power of God and call nations back to faith in God!

God's will is for Jesus to inherit the nations of the earth. As the Son of God, Jesus died so that the world could be returned to the love of the Father and know the Lordship of Christ, who rules with justice, righteousness, and mercy.

God says to us today through Psalms 2:8:
"Ask and the Kingdoms will be your inheritance".

If Jesus as the Son of God is to inherit the nations, we as sons and daughters of God who also cry 'Abba Father', are encouraged to ask for the nations.

We as co-heirs with Christ can cry out for the nations in order to give Jesus the 'inheritance' due His name!

Paul says in Romans 8:15-17,

> 'Instead, you received God's Spirit when he adopted you as his own children. Now we call him, "Abba, Father." For his Spirit joins with our spirit to affirm that we are God's children. And since we are his children, we are his heirs. In fact, together with Christ we are

heirs of God's glory'. (NLT)

Indeed, it is the promise of the Father that Jesus receive the reward of His suffering, the nations of the earth.

Psalms 111:6 declares,

'He reveals mighty power and marvels to his people by handing them nations as a gift'.

In this New Era, God is equipping His church to disciple nations.

God Is Moving His Church From A Position Of Defence To A Position Of Offence

In past times, it has seemed the church has mostly retreated when facing the unrelenting forces of the powers of this world.

Liberal agendas have seemingly marginalized the influence of the church across the nations. The church appeared to back out of society in a desperate hope that Jesus would return and take us from the world that has been overwhelming us.

However, there is an urgent call in the Spirit for the church of Jesus Christ to 'Rise and Shine!'

This generation is no longer happy to try to avoid the onslaught of the enemy.

They are being equipped to stand and take hold of the promises God has given. We have a justice generation rising who are aggressive against the injustice that they see in the world.

This is the heart of the Father and He is raising up His believers to move forward and become change agents who will enforce a whole New Era of His Kingdom rule on the earth.

God Himself is declaring to His church that it is time to get on the front foot and begin to fight, '*30* But Caleb tried to quiet the people as they stood before Moses. "Let's go at once to take the land," he said. "We can certainly conquer it!"

Unfortunately, many nations and people groups languish because they do not live under the Lordship of Christ and the ways of the Kingdom of God. The enemy continues to steal, kill, and destroy peoples and their land, all across the nations.

God is giving us greater revelation, hope and strategy for how we can win and disciple nations. God's plan is to make disciples of nations so that all have the opportunity to know Jesus and thrive under His Lordship in the nations of the earth!

God Considers Nations And People Groups As One Entity

There are many references in scripture in which God refers to nations, people groups and land as individual entities. Throughout the whole Bible, we see God address churches, cities, nations, Kingdoms and even the whole world as one person.

God declares prophetic words through His prophets to each group in the same way we may prophecy over an individual.

In Hosea we see God dealing with all of Israel as one person.

Hosea 2:14-16

'But then I will win her back once again. I will lead her into the desert and speak tenderly to her there. I will return her vineyards to her and transform the Valley of Trouble into a gateway of hope.

'She will give herself to me there, as she did long ago when she was young, when I freed her from her captivity in Egypt. When that day comes," says the Lord "you will call me 'my husband' ...'

In Isaiah 62:4 Isaiah prophesies,

'No longer will they call you Deserted, or name your land Desolate. But you will be called Hephzibah, and your land Beulah; for the Lord will take delight in you, and your land will be married.'

We can find similar examples where God deals with other nations as one individual entity.

- Isaiah 15-16 contains prophecies about Moab.
- Isaiah 17 gives a prophecy directed to Damascus (Syria) and Ephraim (the Northern Kingdom). Isaiah records a prophecy of the destruction of these two nations and some of the destruction's effects upon the two nations.
- Isaiah 18 speaks to the land of Ethiopia.
- Isaiah 19–20 records prophecies about Egypt, which was one of the most powerful nations in the world in Isaiah's day. Isaiah prophesied of ways Egypt would be troubled and how the Egyptians would not be able to

solve their troubles through their own abilities or false gods.

- Isaiah 20 speaks specifically about the time when Assyria would take Egypt captive, warning the people of Judah not the rely on these nations.
- Isaiah 21 speaks about the eventual destruction of three nations: Babylon, Edom and Arabia. [13]

Isaiah was not the only prophet to prophesy over nations.

Jeremiah 1:5 tells us Jeremiah was called as a 'prophet to the nations'.

Ezekiel, Jonah, and Daniel, along with others, were also appointed to prophesy to surrounding nations and speak into them as one entity.

God had compassion on the people of the nations and He used His prophets and watchmen to call them out of unrighteousness and back to Himself so that the people and the land would be blessed.

Today, God is raising up His prophets and watchmen to again call nations into covenant relationship, to free and bless the people.

In Revelation 1:4, we see the Lord giving a message through John to individual churches as one person.

> 'This letter is from John to the seven churches in the province of Asia.'

He again corrects and encourages each one of them as a single person.

We see Isaiah refer to the city of Jerusalem as someone who needs prayer support.

In Isaiah 62:1-2

Because I love Zion, I will not keep still. Because my heart yearns for Jerusalem, I cannot remain silent.

I will not stop praying for her until her righteousness shines like the dawn, and her salvation blazes like a burning torch. The nations will see your righteousness. World leaders will be blinded by your glory.

And you will be given a new name by the Lord's own mouth.

God, through the prophet, refers to the nations of Israel and Judah as sisters that have turned themselves into harlots and abandoned their true love.

In Jeremiah 3:6-8 we read,

'During the reign of King Josiah, the Lord said to me, "Have you seen what fickle Israel has done? Like a wife who commits adultery, Israel has worshiped other gods on every hill and under every green tree. I thought, 'After she has done all this, she will return to me.' But she did not return, and her faithless sister Judah saw this. She saw that I divorced faithless Israel because of her adultery. But that treacherous sister Judah had no fear, and now she, too, has left me and given herself to prostitution'.

These nations, people groups and cites are seen to make their decisions and choices based on an authority structure and a collective conscience developed in the leaders and the nation due to its collective history.

Scripture displays how the decisions of the Kings and leaders in nations brought prosperity or demise to the nation.

Kings who led the nation to follow the precepts of God led the nation into blessing and the nation prospered. The reverse was also true. Where Kings failed to follow God's plans, the nation came into barrenness and we see Israel eventually lose the promised land that they were given.

God again responds to these actions and decisions made by the nations, as if they were one entity.

God Deals With Nations Dependent On Their Actions

God deals with individuals three ways and the same is true again for the nations, people groups and cities.

1) He asks us to surrender to the Lordship of Christ,

2) To do to others as we would have them do to us and

3) Bless Israel that we may be blessed.

Throughout the writings of the prophets we see God dealing with nations, people groups and cities dependent on how they respond to these same 3 things.

1) The Lordship of Christ,

2) The way they deal with other nations and

3) Their relationships and actions toward Israel.

Let's look at each one of these:

1. God calls us to repentance and submission to the Lordship of Christ.

In Ezekiel 25:4 it says,

'The city of Tyre was also reduced to non-existence because of her pride and the fact that she thought she was greater than God'.

God dealt with Tyre because of her pride. In the book of Daniel, He also dealt with King Nebuchadnezzar for the same reason. In Daniel 4, God gives everyone, from individuals to nations, the opportunity to repent. [14]

Just like in Daniel, when we, in our pride and arrogance, cause the oppression of the innocent, then God will rise to protect the innocent and vulnerable. He will stand against evil principalities and powers so the innocent can be freed and those in bondage can be released.

2. God watches how we deal with others.

The book of Jonah, tells of God's compassion on a heathen city. Nineveh was the capitol of the Assyrian Empire that dominated the Middle East at the time of the sacking of Israel. God dealt with Nineveh as an individual. God sent Jonah to ask the King of the nation and the whole city to repent so that he could send a blessing and not destroy them because of their sin and oppression of others. [15]

They repented and the Lord relented, and they were spared.⁽¹⁶⁾

The need for forgiveness, healing and deliverance applies to people groups, whole nations and to the land. God heals and delivers the land, communities and nations as He does individuals.

As 2 Chronicles 4:17 says,

'….forgive their sin and heal their land.'

3. A nation dealing harshly with Israel.

Ezekiel 25:1-4

'Then this message came to me from the Lord: "Son of man, turn and face the land of Ammon and prophesy against its people. Give the Ammonites this message from the Sovereign Lord: Hear the word of the Sovereign Lord! Because you cheered when my Temple was defiled, mocked Israel in her desolation, and laughed at Judah as she went away into exile, I will allow nomads from the eastern deserts to overrun your country"'.

The Ammonites brought destruction on themselves for the way they treated Judah.

However, in this New Testament era, the ruler of this world has already been judged by Jesus.

Jesus, in His death and resurrection, judged the principalities and powers of this world. He then declared that He had given His church the authority over these powers to rule with righteousness and justice in the earth on His behalf. The people of God have authority to release people and nations by the power of the blood of Jesus. There is authority to release forgiveness into a situation, by releasing forgiveness and repenting on behalf of nations and people groups.

However, like King Nebuchadnezzar of the Old Testament and King Herod of the New Testament, if there is a refusal to repent, then we will reap what we have sown.

God himself takes action to rescue the oppressed.

He rides with His army in the heavens and on the earth, the 'ekklesia' of God.

As the 'ekklesia' rise to declare the authority of Jesus and bring down the authority of the powers in the spirit realm, oppression can be lifted.

God has judged the principalities and powers of the earth, and the blood of Jesus has overcome these powers. It is for each person and nation to avail themselves of the sure mercy of God, for He wants all to be saved. Both individuals and nations can choose to live in the benefits of faith in the power of the death and resurrection of Christ.[17]

In the time of Constantine, the large Roman Empire embraced Christianity throughout the empire.[18] Christian nations since that time have also decided to embrace the rule and covenant of Christ.[19]

Even in modern history this is true and today there are some nations and states that have declared they will live by Christian standards. Today, several nations officially identify themselves as Christian states or have state churches, including Argentina, Costa Rica, Denmark (inc. Greenland), Dominican Republic, El Salvador, England, Faroe Islands, Georgia, Greece, Hungary, Iceland, Liechtenstein, Malta, Monaco, Norway, Samoa, Tonga, Tuvalu, Vatican City and Zambia. A Christian state stands in contrast to a secular state, an atheist state, or another religious state, such as a Jewish state, or an Islamic state. [20]

A nation that declares the Lordship of Christ welcomes the Kingdom of Heaven on earth. For these nations there will be longevity and prosperity. America at its founding decided to be a nation that lived under righteous and just laws of the Bible. In doing so, they became a nation that has thrived over the last 200 years. They became one of the most powerful and prosperous nations in the world. Amazingly, Denmark, Norway, and Iceland have these same Christian foundations and all rank in the top most prosperous nations in the earth according to the The Legatum Institute. [21]

As nations build on the righteous and just laws of the Kingdom of God, they will be established firmly as a nation and prosper. The people within that nation will flourish as the nation lives under the just parameters of the Kingdom of God.

Unfortunately, many nations in the West who established themselves on Christian standards during the Reformation and Revival eras of the 1700s and 1800s are now abandoning the standards of Christ and thus courting devastation, as they sow to the wind and reap the whirlwind.[22]

Throughout history, as Israel wandered from the ways of God and followed the ways of the nations which they had conquered, they found themselves devastated. The land no longer produced crops each year, there was war and poverty throughout the nation.(23)

God told Israel to choose life! He begged them to follow His ways for His ways ensured righteous and justice were found in the nation and the people could flourish. He declared that His ways would bring them abundant life.(24)

This is still true for nations today. We are still faced with the same choice of governing our nations with our own 'good ideas' or living by the ways of God's Kingdom.

God has heard the cry of the those suffering injustice and He has heard the cry of the land that has been tainted by innocent blood. He is calling the nations back to the knowledge of Him and His ways. He is calling nations to choose life.

Where these principles are broken, longevity ceases.

Where greed, lust of the flesh and pride of life overtake the rulership of any individual or nation, injustice is the result. When the cries of the innocent are heard in heaven, God will answer. God stepped up to deliver the innocent in the same way He heard the cries of the Israelites and delivered them from Egypt.

God is still hearing the cries and He is calling His ekklesia to rise as did Moses and Aaron and again make His presence felt in the nations, through signs wonders and miracles. God has come to set the oppressed free! God has declared 'mercy' and He has commissioned His 'ekklesia' to declare forgiveness in the nations!

In Isaiah 40, considered by most to be a reflection of the New Testament within Isaiah's writings, God declares:

> Comfort, comfort O my people, speak tenderly to Jerusalem, her harsh days are over! [25]

Pray and cry out for the nations to hear and perceive the forgiveness and freedom of the Kingdom of Heaven freely made available.

Jesus calls nations and individuals to respond to the offer of salvation. A nation who will declare the Lordship of Christ welcomes the Kingdom of Heaven on the earth.

For these nations there will be longevity and prosperity. As they build on righteous and just laws of the Kingdom of God, they will be established firmly as a nation.

CHAPTER 10

Authority to Shift Nations

The Kingdom Of Heaven Is At Hand

God is passionate to see the nations and land thrive, and He is passionate to bring forth nations in righteousness so that the people can live in peace and prosperity!

Jesus Himself said that God is concerned for every sparrow that falls to the ground, and is He not even more concerned about peoples and nations and the land for which they are responsible?

The parameters of individual lives are most often dictated by the righteousness or unrighteousness of the nation in which they live. The laws by which we are governed decide whether an individual will thrive or live under oppression, poverty and injustice.

It is sad for the nation that has leaders who are in power for their own benefit. Scripture declares that where there is greed and selfish ambition there is every kind of sin. [1] When leaders in authority are marked by greed and selfish ambition, the nation and the people will be stripped of justice and fall prey to an unrighteous system that breeds injustice and robs wealth and life from the people.

Where laws have been passed in the land that give licence to the murder of the innocent, we open the doors to a spirit of murder in the nations. We now see violent murder and loss of life across the nations in devastating measure.

God Is After A 'Shift In The Nations'

God is after a change in the collective conscience of every nation so that the nation can thrive and the people flourish.

As with an individual, when a nation surrenders to the authority of Christ, He forgives sins and brings life.

As nations repent and allow Jesus' Lordship to be established in the land, He will forgive their sin and heal their land.

In Joel, we see God dealing with nations. I believe that this is true right now in history. God has His eye on nations. Today's nations are in the valley of decision. I believe God's heart is to bring His people and nations into the restoration of Joel 2:15-32.

This is a *kairos* time now for the nations. God is saying 'Restore'!

He is saying it is the time of the harvest. God is declaring

He has come to rescue the innocent and set free the oppressed!

Nations will rise or fall in this era dependent on how they respond to God, His Kingdom and Israel.

The call to pray for nations is getting louder. The call for the Watchmen to be watching, praying, and making decrees over nations is reverberating in the earth.

There is an army of righteousness that must come forth to call the nations into righteousness.

It is time for nations to turn their heart to follow God's righteous and just laws and acknowledge that they are responsible to a God in heaven.

Authority Of The Ekklesia

God decrees in Isaiah 9:6,

> 'For a child is born to us, a son is given to us. The government will rest on his shoulders. And he will be called: Wonderful Counselor, Mighty God, Everlasting Father, Prince of Peace. His government and its peace will never end. He will rule with fairness and justice from the throne of his ancestor David for all eternity. The passionate commitment of the Lord of Heaven's Armies will make this happen!'

Jesus fulfilled the promise of Isaiah 9:6-7 and has established His governmental rule upon the earth through the nation who is the 'people of God'. The governmental authority in the earth is on His shoulders and He calls us as His 'Ekklesia' to govern in the earth and establish His righteousness and justice through the authority of His name.

As the Kingdom of God is ruled in heaven through the wisdom of righteousness and justice, so Jesus prayed, 'may it be on earth as it is in heaven.' [2] The governmental authority of God has come into the earth through Jesus Christ to command justice for the oppressed and freedom for captives. It is the privilege of God's people as His appointed kings and priests on the earth, to hear the heart and voice of God for nations and people groups, families and communities and begin to enforce righteousness and justice on the earth.

God is calling us as His legislative council to take up the 'Gavel of God' and decree justice into the unjust situations we face!

The sound of the gavel coming down is a sound of His word out of our mouth. It is essential that we call and decree the justice of God into the earth, making way for Heaven to be established on earth!

In this New Era, we must take up our authority and release the power of God through decrees to build heaven upon the earth.

God gave the Israelites power over their enemies so that they could build Him a home upon the earth as an example of what was to come. Jesus then came so that the House of the Lord could be built in us.

He has given us individual power and authority to establish His home in us. He has also given us this power and authority to now establish His home among the nations through His life poured out through each one of His people.

Luke 9:1-3, 5-6 in *The Passion Translation* says,

'Jesus summoned together his twelve apostles and imparted to them authority over every demon and the power to heal every disease. Then he commissioned them to preach God's kingdom realm and to heal the sick to demonstrate that the kingdom had arrived.... The apostles departed and went into the villages with the wonderful news of God's kingdom realm, and they instantly healed diseases wherever they went'.

This is the demonstration of the Kingdom on earth and justice being enforced!

Jesus is summoning His people and again imparting power to demonstrate the authority of the Kingdom for good.

The Power In You To Shift The Heavens And The Earth!

God has placed His authority in us to rule and reign in the earth. He has provided everything we need for life and godliness. As we use all that He has provided, we will reign in this life. God has given each of us much strength and power to do great exploits, for we are called to flourish in this world as Jesus did when He was here.

1. The Power of Entering the Heavenly Realms

I had a recent powerful encounter with the Lord that indicated to me that we are most effective when we operate from out of the heavenly realms. We are seated with Him in heavenly places and it is necessary for us to establish ourselves in this realm.

As I sat in worship, I had a sense of something like an atmosphere clearing before me.

It came until I was inside of it, but at the very edge. I sensed I was on the edge of Heaven. There was a sound like the sound that I had heard others talk of, who had been at the edge of heaven.

I felt the Lord say, 'The mist has been rolled away.' I sensed now I was able to see clearly into heaven.

As I looked, I saw that I was up high in a large bank of clouds. As I looked down, there was what I perceived to be the city of God. It was golden and full of light that was emanating from it. It appeared to be in the centre of this heavenly realm.

There seemed to be an angel with me and although I didn't really see him, he took me down into the city.

The first place we went was the temple. Everything was golden. We went straight into the courtyard and then stopped on the steps between the porch and the altar (the place of intercession). After some time there, the angel indicated we were going on.

He took me outside to the left of the temple and straight into the Courthouse of heaven.

Here, Jesus was the judge and He was holding court. This was His courtroom and He was Chief Justice.

He indicated that He would expect to see me here often, legislating for justice upon the earth.

After a little time, it seemed the Spirit said, 'I have one more place to take you and this is where you will spend more and more of your time, until you spend most of your time here.' With this the angel ushered me into the 'The Throne Room.'

God the Father was on the throne and He motioned that I should come closer. Then He said, 'Come right up on My lap and sit with Me.' He reminded me that 'even the sparrows make a nest for themselves here around the Father's throne.'

After a little time, I hopped off His lap and stood beside the throne. I felt like a child just standing with her daddy.

After a little while, it seemed that it was time for me to go. As I turned, the Father said, 'Don't forget to take something with you from the throne room so that you have everything you need.' I looked around and saw that there was what looked like a stockpile of gold bullion bars stacked up behind the throne. I took two, but the Lord indicated I should take more. So, I took another one. Then He looked at me, like He was thinking about something and loaded me up with two more, indicating that I would now have enough.

The angel then escorted me back to the edge of heaven. I had a strong sense that these three places in heaven were now where God expected me to spend much of my time.

This encounter is important to help understand the heavenly realm and the vital need to work with the heavenly realm to enforce heaven on earth. The vision describes the mist as now rolled back, indicating that greater revelation of the Kingdom of Heaven is being opened in this New Era.

We often quote that we are 'seated in heavenly places'. [3] The Lord is making this a greater reality. He is releasing greater knowledge of the realm of heaven and how we are to operate from this realm. In fact, to see Jesus' prayers that it be, 'on earth as it is in heaven,' it will be necessary to understand very well how heaven operates.

As prayer warriors and intercessors, there is a call into the place of intercession. It is a privilege to join Jesus as He lives in the place of intercession, His blood making a way in the spiritual realm.[4]

As kings and priests who serve their God, the warriors find themselves in the place of making decrees from the Courts of Heaven. As ones seated in heavenly places, as legislators with legal authority in the heavenly realm, in the court we present cases and release the decrees given. On behalf of the court we ensure these declarations and judgements of the Kingdom are decreed on the earth. [5] There are examples of decrees in Appendix 2 of this book.

As worshippers, we are found in the throne room worshipping and understanding how a king operates by being in the presence of the King of Kings. In the Throne Room, time is spent in worship, receiving what is necessary to bring to earth from heaven. In this place there is access to the necessary wealth, in all its facets, that is needed to extend the Kingdom on earth.

There is much teaching on the gift of prayer and our position between the porch and the altar, where intercession was made in the Old Testament temple. There has been a lot of new teaching on the courts of heaven in recent times. It is another immensely powerful revelation to be mastered. The release of prayer through accessing the Throne Room of God and His glory is yet to be fully explored.

The Lord spoke to me and whispered, *'Everything you need you will find in the glory!'* We have found this to be true as we have explored the effect of worship that takes us into the glory realm, has had on our prayers for the nations.

God is inviting us into the heavenly realms to understand more of how heaven operates. When we understand heaven, then we can effectively release heaven to earth. It is our delight and privilege to take up the authority that God has given us to release His Kingdom in the earth.

2. The Power of the Covenant and Communion

When, by faith, we agree and submit to the authority of Heaven, God promises us a covenant commitment. Through the power of Covenant there is access to the authority of Heaven, for individuals, regions and the nations.

Jesus Himself is the guarantee of the new covenant.

Revelation 5:9

'And they were all singing this new song of praise to the Lamb:
Because you were slaughtered for us, you are worthy to take the scroll and open its seals. Your blood was the price paid to redeem us. You purchased us to bring us to God *out of every tribe, language, people group, and nation*'.

In 1 Samuel 5, The Philistines capture the Ark of God. The Ark was a symbol of God's first covenant with His people and His presence among them. When this symbol of the covenant of God was brought into the temple of Dagon, Dagon was powerless against it.

1 Samuel 5:2

'They carried the Ark of God into the temple of Dagon and placed it beside an idol of Dagon. But when the citizens of Ashdod went to see it the next morning, Dagon had fallen with his face to the ground in front of the Ark of the Lord! So they took Dagon and put him in his place again. But the next morning the same thing happened—Dagon had fallen face down before the Ark of the Lord again. This time his head and hands had broken off and were lying in the doorway'.

When the people of God come into covenant with the greater authority of Christ and carry the power and presence of Christ, the idols of the land will fall. They will fall at the threshold or entrance (i.e. gates) of their jurisdiction, just as happened with the old covenant. It is from this place, at the threshold, the gate, that another authority can then be established in that place. This enforces a shift of power where the authority of the powers of darkness can be broken and the authority of Christ established.

When there is agreement to come into covenant with Jesus, we, His Ark, can carry His authority into a location. Through the authority of Christ, powers that have usurped Christ's authority and occupied that territory can be dethroned. Therefore, we can rise and take spiritual authority in an area. Everywhere our feet tread, by alignment with the authority of the covenant, the authority of the enemy can be shifted out of the land! [3]

It is through communion with the body and blood of Jesus that we enter into covenant with the Lord. Communion appropriates the power of the blood over and over in us so that we can stand in the forgiveness, wholeness and righteousness of the life of Jesus and His resurrection power.

When we have communion, we enforce the authority of Jesus in our life as our King and Saviour. As we align our own lives under the authority of the covenant of Christ, we can use this authority to shift the spiritual realm over a region. As ambassadors of the Kingdom of Heaven, we have authority to possess territory on Heaven's behalf. Again, this has application from a personal level to a regional and national level.

When a territory is taken on behalf of another authority, often symbols are erected to make known this authority. The use of acts and symbols to mark someone's authority in an area is common. Most often today, nations use flags to declare their authority in a region. These symbols are also recognised in the spiritual realm. In other instances, statues are erected, or plaques mounted.

As ambassadors of the Kingdom of Heaven, we can symbolically pour out the wine of communion, a symbol of the covenant we have with heaven, as an act of declaring the authority of Christ in a region. This act is recognised in the spiritual realm, enforcing the Covenant and therefore, the Lordship of Jesus is declared for that region.

The power of the blood and the decrees of the saints enthrone Jesus in that territory and enforce His Kingdom authority over it. We ratify the covenant through declarations that ensure the shift in the spirit is secured, and Jesus is now Lord in that place.

3. Power of the Blood and Forgiveness

Scripture tells us that Jesus overcame all the power of evil in the earth, the heavens and under the earth. [6] Jesus overcame through the sacrifice of His body and His shed blood on the cross. His blood offers forgiveness for the sins of the whole earth.[7]

The authority of His blood shed for us rests in the authority of His blood offered in Heaven. Hebrews 6:19 says,

> 'We have this certain hope like a strong, unbreakable anchor holding our souls to God himself. Our anchor

of hope is fastened to the mercy seat which sits in the heavenly realm beyond the sacred threshold'.

Jesus' blood is presented in the heavenly tabernacle and declares forgiveness in the heavens and on the earth. Jesus is our forever priest, offering the shed blood of His own sacrifice, sprinkled on the altar to forgive the sins of all who call on Him.

Hebrews 7:28

'The law appointed flawed men as high priests, but God's promise, sealed with his oath, which succeeded the law, appoints a perfect Son who is complete forever!'

In Jesus' time on earth, He used the power of forgiveness to heal a paralysed man.

Luke 5:19-22

'So they went up to the roof and took off some tiles. Then they lowered the sick man on his mat down into the crowd, right in front of Jesus. Seeing their faith, Jesus said to the man, "Young man, your sins are forgiven".

'But the Pharisees and teachers of religious law said to themselves, "Who does he think he is? That's blasphemy! Only God can forgive sins!"'

'Jesus knew what they were thinking, so he asked them, "Why do you question this in your hearts? Is it easier to say 'Your sins are forgiven,' or 'Stand up and walk'? So I will prove to you that the Son of Man has the authority on earth to forgive sins." Then Jesus turned to the paralysed man and said, "Stand up, pick up your mat, and go home!"

Jesus offers forgiveness and healing undifferentiated, to a paraplegic. He said to those who questioned Him that He could either declare the forgiveness of sin or declare that this man was healed. The two apparently were interchangeable.

He offered this authority to the disciples through the Holy Spirit which He breathed upon them, before returning to heaven.

In John 20:22-23 after Jesus had risen from the dead, He declared to the disciples they now had this same authority to forgive sin.

'Then he breathed on them and said, "Receive the Holy Spirit. If you forgive anyone's sins, they are forgiven. If you do not forgive them, they are not forgiven."'

The declaration of forgiveness over people, families, cities and nations has great power in the spirit to release healing. When we offend or sin against someone, we ask forgiveness. When forgiveness is offered, it heals and restores our souls to know we are forgiven.

Likewise, it appears bodies also can be made whole through the power of forgiveness available through the blood. The authority of the blood to forgive is our inheritance.

In Genesis 4:8-12 (ESV), the story is told of Cain killing Abel. Scripture records that the Lord said to Cain,

'The voice of your brother's blood is crying to me from the ground. And now you are cursed from the ground, which has opened its mouth to receive your brother's blood from your hand. When you work the ground, it shall no longer yield to you its strength. You shall be a fugitive and a wanderer on the earth." What have you done? Listen! Your brother's blood cries out to me from the ground!'

When blood is unrighteously taken, the people live under a curse. The land also which received the blood now becomes unproductive. It is contaminated and no longer flourishes as it normally would.

We have seen this across the nations as the earth groans under the weight of sin. It is crying out for the sons and daughters of God to rise in their authority and reverse the curse that has come upon the land. [8]

When the land needs healing and restoration, the blood of Jesus and the power of forgiveness in the blood 'speaks a better word'. It has the power to heal and restore the land, covering the land with forgiveness and breaking the curse of barrenness and death.

The release of forgiveness has power through the blood to release the people and the land from a curse. [9]

From the cross Jesus declared forgiveness, acknowledging that the people had no idea what they were doing. We also can pronounce forgiveness through the blood of Jesus.

Forgiveness is a powerful spiritual weapon yielding great results when used at the direction of the Holy Spirit.

Jesus says to take communion often to remember Him and the work of His overcoming authority in our lives. The power of the blood of Jesus cleanses us from sin and we are renewed. The blood of Jesus poured out and forgiveness declared in a place or on the land, has the power to sanctify and cleanse that place.

4. Revelation of the Names of God

It is a vital necessity for us, as we press in to shift nations, to also know who God is in greater dimensions. As has been mentioned, Moses needed the revelation of I AM to shift the people of Israel from under the government of Pharaoh and into a new understanding of the government of God under which they now lived.

As we receive greater revelation and have a greater relationship with the Godhead, we can release by faith a greater dimension of His authority. When God's names are declared in all the many aspects of who He is, it releases greater dimensions of His authority, presence, and power on earth.

The declaration of His names releases authority that powerfully shifts the realm of the spirit. Authority in the spiritual realm can be changed as the names of God are decreed at the gate, heart and hill of a nation. The hordes of the enemy that have taken residence in a territory recognise the power of the names of God and the authority of Christ to depose them.

God is always looking for a man or woman on earth who will agree with Him. "I looked for a man to stand in the gap before for the land, but I found no one…". (10)

As people born on the earth, we have authority in the earth realm, and God asks us to stand in this authority to bring heaven to earth. (11)

5. The Power of Fasting to Shift Nations

As my husband Bruce Lindley says, 'National corporate prayer and fasting shifts nations.'

This has been true in our experience.

In scripture, there are many examples of the way fasting adds authority for breakthrough over the power of the enemy. Daniel, Esther, Jesus and the disciples all used the power of fasting. Lou Engle teaches that fasting gives an explosive power to our prayers that can change the course of history!

When Jesus encountered the little boy who was afflicted by a demon, he told His disciples, *'This type does not come out except through prayer and fasting.'* There are many 'types' of powers and principalities that we encounter that can only be shifted through the power of fasting.

In the moment Jesus spoke this He was not fasting, but He had previously fasted. He had fasted for 40 days in the wilderness in preparation for His ministry. It was in this place that He overcame many of the powers of the enemy he was about to encounter. As such, when He encountered this enemy, he was able to overcome.

The same is true while preparing for a prayer strike. In fasting and prayer much is overcome before the prayer strike has begun. Then, when worship and decrees are made, it is done with the authority that has already been established.

The definition of, 'to fast' means 'to wage war.' [12] When we oppose principalities and powers, fasting brings another weapon to our warfare. Experience shows that fasting releases greater revelation for our assignment, unlocks hidden understanding, and gives clearer strategy for the battle. Time and again the power of fasting has led to a to shift in a situation that before had seemed impossible to be changed.

Fasting denies the physical so that the spiritual realm can more clearly come into focus and the power and authority of God can be displayed more fully to and through His people on the earth. We do not fast to twist God's arm to move on our behalf. We fast to empower ourselves to rise in the authority already given us, overcoming the power of our own doubts and unbelief.

Lou Engle amplified Alfred Lord Tennyson's famous quote, declaring, 'More is wrought through prayer *and fasting* than ever this world dreamed.'

Rule In The Midst Of Your Enemies

Psalm 110:1-2

'Yahweh said to my Lord, the Messiah:
"Sit with me as enthroned ruler while I subdue your every enemy.

They will bow low before you as I make them a footstool for your feet".

Messiah, I know God himself will establish your kingdom as you reign in Zion-glory.

For he says to you, "Rule in the midst of your enemies!

Your people will be your love offerings,

In the day of your mighty power you will be exalted,

and in the brightness of your holy ones you will shine

as an army arising from the womb of the dawn".

In this Psalm, God is addressing Jesus and encouraging Him to rule in the midst of His enemies and stating that He (God) would do the fighting for Him. We as the army of God will rise and shine as the Lord fights to establish His Kingdom on earth.

I keep hearing the Lord encouraging His people, with the same encouragement.

'Rule in the midst of your enemies!'

Jesus in His time on earth declared His authority over the smallest things — the loaves and fish.

Luke 9:17 says,

'So everyone ate until they were filled, and afterward the disciples gathered up the leftovers—it came to exactly twelve baskets full!'

Jesus also declared His authority over the greatest of things in the earth — the wind and waves.

In Matthew 8:27 it says,

> 'The disciples were astonished by this miracle and said to one another, "Who is this Man? Even the wind and waves obey His word."'

He then imparted this authority to His disciples as He commanded them to disciple the nations.
Matthew 28:18-19 says,

> 'Then Jesus came close to them and said, "All the authority of the universe has been given to me. Now go in my authority…"'

In March 2019 God told me that the 'Gavel of God' had come into the earth to judge against injustice! I saw that God was putting this gavel in a greater dimension into the hands of His people to decree His victory over injustice everywhere we see it.

It is unjust for people to not live in total victory because Jesus paid the price for all the earth to be released from the slavery of sin and its effect on the land.

Our authority is only compromised by our mindsets and the lies we believe.

These lies limit our hope and faith. God is releasing revelation and power in this New Era, so that His people take up His authority and rule in the midst of their enemies.

He is adjusting our mindsets. He is delivering us from the restrictive attitudes and unbelief that have prevented us from being effective and left us unable to overcome the power of the enemy in our lives and those around us.

Luke 9:41, 44 (TPT)

'Jesus responded, "You are an unbelieving people with no faith! Your lives are twisted with lies that have turned you away from doing what is right. How much longer should I remain here, offering you hope?" Then he said to the man, "Bring your son to me."'

God is calling us aside to rise out of unbelief and freely take up our authority and rule in the midst of our enemies!

The Call To Disciple Nations

God would not ask His people to disciple nations unless it were possible. With the coming of the new apostolic era, the church/ekklesia is gaining the insight and authority to begin to function in a way that will impact nations. God is wanting nations and people groups to flourish under His hand and free people from the oppression they currently live under.

In Matthew 29:18-20, Jesus commissions the people of God to baptize and disciple nations across the earth and bring them into the governance of the Kingdom of God.

In this New Era, God is calling nations to rise and live by His standards. He is calling leaders of nations back to the ways of Kingdom righteousness and justice. God is calling whole nations to again rise and call themselves Christian nations in more than just name.

God is calling forth the body of Christ to rise up and lead

nations in spheres of influence to enforce righteousness and justice in every sector of society. He is changing our perspective to see each nation and people group as an entity. He is releasing us to prophesy to nations and pray for nations, regions and whole people groups. He is also calling nations and people groups to know their calling and identity as nations set apart for the purposes of God.

Jesus, when on earth, sent His disciples to bring individuals to Him. He also called and equipped them to disciple the communities in the earth, to live in the ways of Heaven. This is how the newly formed church flourished across the Roman empire and beyond in the first century.

In 2 Corinthians 11:28, we see Paul labouring over his concern for the churches that he had established across the cities and nations. The Kingdom continued to move forward, seeing whole cities and nations shift under the Lordship of Christ. The understanding of the gospel, the ways of God and the government of God, spread all over the then known world. The truth of the gospel was seen and its ability to impact cities and nations was made obvious.

Apostles of this new era began to establish new centres of Godly government. [13]

Unfortunately, by the time of Constantine, although nations began to live in the light of the gospel, it melded into the culture of the day. Slowly, the gospel became completely compromised and hidden for the most part, as the world was plunged into the dark ages.

However, the light of the gospel, which can never be put out, came forth again in a New Era of Enlightenment that blossomed into the Reformation of the 1500s. God continued to work across the nations and through His people, and more and more of God's truth and His ways were uncovered. These truths flourished in the time of the Wesleyan Revival of the 1700s in England.

Nations across England and Europe at this time began to understand the Bible and the laws of the 10 Commandments became the basis of their legal systems. Whole nations adopted Christian values. [14]

European nations were experiencing revival and many missionaries were thrust out into the nations to release the knowledge of the Kingdom of heaven on earth. Throughout Europe, and in the newly established Americas, reformed governments established themselves with Christian laws, morals and values.

In England, by the 1800s the slave trade was halted. The age of consent was increased and child labour was abolished. The institution of nursing was birthed. Education became mandatory and many other practices of today were set in motion. Many nations established themselves as 'Christian' and aligned themselves with the laws set out in the Bible, establishing many nations on righteous and just laws. These nations are now considered 'western nations' or first world nations. [15]

Unfortunately, since the time of the World Wars, the laws and precepts of God in Christian nations have been eroded away. Many historical happenings have shifted the hearts and minds of men. Mindsets and heartaches have allowed deception into the nations and opened doors for other rulers of this world to take control of the laws of nations.

These laws have opposed the righteousness of God and we are seeing western nations sinking into a culture that opposes Christ and His people. It is a culture resulting in death and destruction rather than life!

God is still calling nations and people groups to choose 'life!' God is making a way where we see no way to shift nations and peoples under the rule of the government of God.

CHAPTER 11

Shifting Nations

God is wanting to shift people and nations out of the chaos and moral and social decline that we see them spiralling into. God wants to bless the nations, and His ways are the perfect ways for people, regions and nations to live. His ways ensure fairness for all and the blessings of increase and abundant life! [1]

God is the God of nations. God's heart is for the nations. He is the Father of the nations!

God is wanting cities and nations to be ruled in justice and righteousness so the people may flourish.

However, just like individuals, a nation cannot be completely righteous simply by following righteous laws. Righteous laws bring justice and fairness, protection, peace and prosperity into a nation, but simply keeping the law does not provide true freedom from sin.

Israel's history has shown that to us. History continues to repeat itself as we see men's hearts waver from love and devotion to God and, as such, move away from His precepts.

As a nation, Israel went to the greatest heights of any nation when King Solomon was on the throne. They enjoyed great wealth and the favour of the nations, but the sin of man left them vulnerable to the attacks of the enemy within. The king himself turned from righteous ways, and ultimately, the nation lost the blessing of God.[2]

The question must be asked: Are we able to shift a nation into righteousness in the same way we shift a person into righteousness?

If we have been called to disciple nations, then it must be true that we can shift the spiritual authority of a nation from under the rule of darkness into the rule of the authority of heaven.

God has a strategy to do this.

A Strategy To Shift The Spiritual Authority Over Nations And Territories

The first opportunity our Firehouse had to 'shift a nation' arose when we were asked to respond to a request to lead strategic prayer for a nation.

Our first 'Shift the Nation' – Cambodia

In 2011, Cambodia became the first nation in which God

unfolded a strategy for the transition of a whole nation. He taught us how to do this by giving us a prayer assignment.

There were several ministries working together in Cambodia at the time. They had all been alerted to the open trafficking of children on the streets at the northern border of Cambodia into Thailand. Together these ministries actioned a plan to support the government in their desire to stop this trafficking of children out of the nation.

Patricia King of XP Ministries was very heavily involved in the area. There were many being saved and already some children rescued, and Patricia asked us to come and undergird the whole situation in prayer.

We were immediately aware that this assignment meant we would have to understand and pray for the nation and that God was calling us to lift a whole nation to him in prayer.

History and Culture of Cambodia

Cambodia is a nation steeped in Buddhism and tormented by fear. It has at the centre of its culture the largest Buddhist temple in the world We were somewhat overwhelmed as we began to understand the spiritual forces and strongholds that were at play in this nation.

However, as we prayed, God began to release to us a new strategy, that caused faith to rise instead of fear and intimidation.

The Lord began to speak to us about 'Enthroning Jesus over the Nation.' We saw that every nation on the earth is His!

Deuteronomy 10:14

'To the Lord your God belong the heavens, even the highest heavens, the earth and everything in it.'

We understood we could decree His ownership and Lordship across the nation.

Revelation Of The Heart, The Hill And The Gates Of A Nation

The Lord then directed us to a specific strategy of how to do this. The Holy Spirit directed us to enthrone Jesus at three different locations in Cambodia which we later understood to be, the heart (Ankgor Wat), the hill of government (Phnom Wat) and 'the gate' (Poipet, the town on the border of Cambodia and Thailand).

Biblical Understanding

Praying and declaring Jesus' Lordship at the gates, the heart and the hill, caused us to understand that this is the strategy that applies to the individual who gives their heart to Jesus and declares that He is Lord of their life. God began to show us that we could work with and pray for a nation to come into salvation in the same way we pray with individuals.

Romans 10:9 (NLT) says,
'If you openly declare that Jesus is Lord and believe in your heart that God raised him from the dead, you will be saved.'

We give Jesus authority in our lives by believing with our heart. We then choose with our minds to agree with His truth (hill of government, places of political power). We then make a declaration with our mouth (gates) that we have made Jesus the Lord of our life. At this point Christ makes a spiritual transaction with us and we are 'saved.' There is a spiritual transaction because of what is believed in the heart, agreed with in the mind and then decreed through the mouth.

When this transaction is completed, God by the power of His spirit, then transfers us from the Kingdom of darkness into the Kingdom of Light, the Kingdom of Heaven.

Proverbs 18:21 says,

'The tongue can bring death or life; those who love to talk will reap the consequences.'

This transaction can also be true concerning a nation. We have already established that God deals with nations the same way he deals with individuals. Therefore, by believing at the heart, (the spiritual and emotional heart of the nation), agreeing with the mind, (the hill, the high place of authority of government), and declaring Jesus Lordship at the mouth, (the nation's gates), a spiritual transaction can be made in a nation.

Just like an individual, a nation can be moved from under the spiritual authority of the Kingdom of darkness to rulership of Kingdom of Light!

The spiritual authority over a nation can be shifted under the Lordship of Christ! In fact, the heart, the hill, and the gates are all spiritual gateways and as we confess the Lordship of Christ at each place, it brings a powerful transaction in the spirit realm.

> Psalm 24:7 (TPT)
>
> 'So wake up, you living gateways! Lift up your heads, you ageless doors of destiny!
>
> 'Welcome the King of Glory, for he is about to come through you'.

Here scripture declares that we possess gateways and doors of destiny that can open in us. Scripture asks us to use these gates and doors to let the King of Glory in. Likewise, we can use the gateways and doors of a nation to open to the King of Glory! These gateways and doors are the spiritual entryways to an individual, a community, a state, and indeed a nation.

This process of believing, agreeing and confessing with your mouth is true for any transaction in life. Business transactions, social agreements, legal documentation etc., are all based on a declared and witnessed agreement.

For example, a marriage is a public declaration of what you have agreed to. What we believe, (i.e.: that we love and want to marry another person) is declared out of our mouth, then signed and witnessed on a document.

Legal agreements of any type are agreed upon by individuals who have given verbal consent. It is then made valid by the signing and witness of another person or multiple people.

In Old Testament times, written agreements were not available, so other demonstrations were used.

In the book of Ruth, Boas declared he had legally acquired Ruth's land and her hand in marriage at the gate of the city. He did this by following the common custom of legal agreement. He declared his agreement at the gate and ratified it by giving the sandal from his foot. [3]

These transactions and agreements all become binding in the spirit through our spoken words. It is only after the spoken word that it is confirmed by an act dictated by the situation and culture in which it is made. A spiritual agreement is no different. God makes a covenant with us when we believe in the shed blood of Jesus Christ, acknowledge His Lordship in our lives and make a confession to that end.

We can translate this to any region and nation by finding the heart, the hill of government and gates of the region and establishing agreement in the spiritual realm.

When there is agreement with those in authority in the land, declarations that shift a nation can be made. With the agreement of the spiritual, the political and the indigenous authority in the land, a spiritual transaction can be made.

When all three agree to enthrone Jesus and declare Him as the Lord of a nation, this can be enforced in the spiritual realm at the strategic locations of a nation. Through declarations and confessions, a nation is shifted out of the spiritual dominance of the kingdom of darkness into the Kingdom of Light.

When an individual gives their heart to Jesus, they are immediately saved. However, after the decision of salvation, there is a continuation of a process of salvation. A newly saved person doesn't necessarily look or even immediately behave any differently from what they did before they were saved. However, with Jesus' forgiveness and Lordship in their lives, they are taken from glory to glory.

The same is true for nations and people groups. Initially, we may not see too much of a change, but change will come as we continue to enthrone Jesus over that nation.

Jesus' mandate for the body of Christ was to disciple nations. A great beginning is to first shift the spiritual climate over the nation. We can spiritually bring salvation to a nation by bringing it under the Lordship of Christ. In this way we are 'preparing the way of the Lord' so that Jesus is given authority over the nation to bring the land, the seven mountains of society and the peoples into the fullness of salvation.

At the Gate

The gateway, gates and doorways of any region and nation are the demarcation line and boundary for the governmental and judicial authority in that territory.

Those who have authority at the gate have access to the city. When you have access at the gate, you have authority to allow in and out of that territory whatever you desire.

Jesus declared Himself to be the gateway for the sheep. Jesus is our access to abundant life. [4] He is the gateway. He is the authority that gives us access to the realm of eternal and abundant life in Him. It is this authority that we exercise at the nation's gate.

Jesus' blood is the authority by which we enter the heavenly realm. Through believing in the power of the blood of Jesus and by applying Jesus' blood on the gateway of our hearts, through this covenant we give Jesus access and authority in that place. [5]

In Egypt, the blood of the lamb applied on doors declared the Lord's authority and protection on that home. The blood of Jesus at the gates declares He has taken authority there and He is Lord of that territory. [6]

It is clear that the 'gates' of any area is where the spiritual authority and access to that territory lies.

In the Song of Deborah, Deborah declares that Israel had left their God and now they had to fight to re-establish their authority in the land, and yet they seemed powerless.

Judges 5:8

'When Israel chose new gods, war erupted at the city gates. Yet not a shield or spear could be seen among forty thousand warriors in Israel!'

She declared the fight to establish Israel back under the authority of the real God was at the gates. She understood in the spiritual realm that a fight was already happening between the spiritual forces of Heaven's army and the enemy attempting to gain control again in the land of Israel. This fight was at the spiritual 'gate' of the nation. This was the place that authority over the nation could be lost or won.

The actual battle that Deborah initiated between Barak

and his army and Sisera and the forces of the enemy that were oppressing Israel was fought on the plains. However, spiritually, Deborah identified the spiritual authority to rule a territory at the spiritual gate.

In Joshua 6, the first act of taking the promised land was to bring down the city walls and gates of Jericho to get access to the city and therefore authority over the city. [7]

In ancient times, the gates to a city were vital because without them, raiders could come and ransack a city at will. This is why many chose to come and live within the cities and towns. The gates and walls protected the people and ensured safety. If the gates or wall was breached, access to the city was sure.

When Nehemiah heard that the gates of the city of Jerusalem were in disrepair and the people were being stolen from, he was devastated. He begged the king to release him to return to Jerusalem to help repair the walls.

In a miraculous way, God enabled Nehemiah to rebuild the walls and gates of the city. The enemy was vicious against this rebuilding and used many tactics to attempt to distract and stop the project from being completed. Once the gates were established, the city was re-established as the city of God. [8]

The enemy is just as determined today to prevent the repair of the gates and walls in the lives of individuals, cities and nations. When God instructs us to attempt any project to re-establish His authority in any person, home, and territory, it is important to be aware that there will be pushback from the enemy. It is a spiritual battle — we do not fight against flesh and blood. Remember it is the forces of the enemy that are at work, in attempting to prevent God's authority being established.

Be bold and very courageous, God will fight for you.

As has been said in Psalms 24:7, we are encouraged to take up the authority that God has given us.

'So wake up, you living gateways!
Lift up your heads, you ageless doors of destiny!
Welcome the King of Glory,
for he is about to come through you'.

The Lord comes into the earth through the gates that we fling open to Him by the authority He gives us and by the decrees of our mouth. Words declared in faith make way for the King of Glory to come and invade the spiritual atmosphere we occupy. As Jesus is enthroned spiritually, everything in the natural must come into alignment with His authority.

There are many scripture references that speak to the fact that we can make legal transactions in the spirit at the gates.

In Bible times, the elders, those in authority in the city, sat in the gates to make transactions for the city and nation. We see Boaz do that when he bought Ruth's land from a closer relative, therefore making a transaction that included both the land and Ruth. [9]

Samson took the gates of Gaza, gaining access to the city. He overcame the powers at the gate of the city. [10]

Watchmen who watch at city gates and at watch towers over

nations use their positions of authority at the gate to allow in and out of the region what God has authorized. We have seen how vital it is to have the Watchmen watching at the gateways of nations to be alert for the activity in the spiritual realm and what that means for the earth.

Those who have authority at the gate have authority to grant access to the city, territory, region, state or nation. Dark powers and rulers have usurped the authority of Jesus at multiple gates across nations. However, when Jesus' authority at the gate is established, the Kingdom of Heaven has access into the earth from that place. This gives great opportunity in the spiritual realm to release the Kingdom of Heaven to earth.

At the Heart

As Proverbs 15:28 says,

'As a man thinks in his heart so is he.'

How a nation 'thinks' defines the culture and attitudes of a nation. It is the reason different nations may prioritize different events, celebrate different festivals and spend finance in ways differently from another nation. It defines how a nation presents itself to the world and what alignments it has with other nations.

The 'heart' is a collective belief in a set of values and mindsets that we champion as important. These mindsets define who we are and the culture in which we live.

The 'heart' represents a shared mindset, shaped by a nation's heritage and future ambitions. A great example in Australia is the legendary ANZAC mindset that declares their values of courage, endurance, mateship and sacrifice. These are at the core of the nation's mindset and the values by which the military trains their men.[11]

Scripture demonstrates the power of a nation's collective mindset in several examples. Joshua 1:10 shows how 40 years in the wilderness shaped the heart of the children of Israel. Israel was a nation of slaves who had been recently delivered from the clutches of Egypt. They were so intimidated and fearful of the nations around them, they refused to go up against them and fight for their promises.

However, after forty years in the wilderness, we see a nation changed by their collective experience. When Joshua delivered the news that it was now time to take the promised land, no one objected, all were now ready to go up and fight.

There has been a similar shift in the culture of the Church of Jesus Christ on the earth today. Many experienced the wonderful power of the Holy Spirit displayed in the Charismatic era. Unfortunately, even with awakenings like the Argentinian Revival, Toronto and Pensacola, the people of God largely remained intimidated by the power of the enemy. The culture and mindset were to bunker down until Jesus came back to rescue us. Today I see a new landscape and mindset across the body of Christ. In this New Era, there is a call to go up and take the promises that God has given us. I see a generation ready for the fight!

In 1 King's 18, Elijah's show down with the prophets of

Baal shifted Israel's mindset. They went from a nation that was unsure of who their God was to a nation that declared, 'The Lord, He is God.'

In many nations, there is often an event that has happened at a particular place that people can look back on and see that it was instrumental in forging the mindset and heartbeat of a nation.

When we went to pray for the nation of Uganda, we were told of Uganda's history. In the 16th century when missionaries first came, many young men were saved. They were passionate for Christ. Many of these young men were employed by the king of one of the most powerful tribes in the nation. Unfortunately, he misunderstood their zeal, which resulted in the massacre of more than 400 young men who were martyred for Christ.

This left an indelible mark on the heart of the nation. Every year since, the nation closes to celebrate these young men who gave their lives to establish the gospel in Uganda.

The Lord showed us that this was the heart of the nation.

In Cambodia, the Lord made clear that Angkor Wat (Cambodia's large temple, a symbol on their flag) represented the heart of the nation. It was at the core of the nation's historical identity.

Although the collective heart of any nation is so much more than one place or one event, there is often a core place that can represent the heartbeat of the nation. It is a strategic marker that gives the people identity and declares to them a sense of belonging.

Our heart defines who we are. The same is true of a nation, and a nation's heart can be turned to God. America is the prime example of a nation who was established with a heart for God. 'One nation under God', 'In God we trust!' (12)

What is spoken from the mouth reflects what is truly in the heart.

Jesus said in Luke 6:45,

'A good man brings good things out of the good stored up in his heart, and an evil man brings evil things out of the evil stored up in his heart. For the mouth speaks what the heart is full of. **Out of the abundance of the heart the mouth speaks**'.

Matthew 6:21
'For where your treasure is, there your heart will be also'.

Proverbs 4:2-3
'Above all else, guard your heart, for everything you do flows from it'.

And Deuteronomy 30:14 says,
'No, the word is very near you; it is in your mouth and in your heart so you may obey it'.

When believers, leaders and indigenous representatives agree together to decree that the heart of the nation belongs to Jesus and rise to declare Jesus Lordship in the nation, a very powerful shift can take place.

At the Hill

In scripture, the hill or high place is both a natural and spiritual place of authority.

God Himself establishes His authority on earth from the high places like Mount Zion, Mount Sinai, Mount Ebal, Mount Gerizim and the mountains of Jerusalem.

Traditionally, 'The Hill', or the highest point of authority in a nation, was at the highest geographical location in the territory. Kings and rulers set their palaces at these high places where they were most easily protected. It was also a place from which you could survey all that you sought to govern. In ancient nations it was the place of the King's throne where he and his officials enacted laws and governed the nation.

The enemy will attempt to establish himself in the high places, both physical and spiritual, to usurp God's authority in a territory.

> Deuteronomy 12:2
>
> 'When you drive out the nations that live there, you must destroy all the places where they worship their gods—high on the mountains, up on the hills, and under every green tree.'

The 'Hill' of a nation from which the nation is governed today is most often the Federal government or the place of governmental authority in that nation. It is usually the houses of government where elected officials govern the nation. Even today, many nation's capitals and federal authorities are strategically placed on a physical hill.

The nation is governed through the collective mindsets of individuals elected to rule the land. The governmental authority provides opportunity for the collective heart and mindset of a nation to be outworked. This outworking can either align under God's righteous guidelines or reject these righteous laws.

'The Hill' is the place of decision making. In the spiritual realm it is a highly contended place. The power of the enemy will contend at the hill as he does at the gate of a territory to gain access and influence. The Kingdom of God has a plan to rule the nations, but the kingdom of darkness likewise will fight for the heart, hill and gates of a nation. When he has influence and authority in these places, he enforces his evil agenda.

The good news is that Jesus has defeated the enemy, and the nations are His inheritance. It is our privilege to 'make way for the King' to take His rightful place in spiritual leadership of a nation. The power base of a nation can be altered through shifts in spiritual powers in high places. As this is enforced, it will bring influence on the spiritual, soul and physical landscape of a nation.

> Romans 10:9 (NLT)
> 'If you openly declare that Jesus is Lord and believe in your heart that God raised him from the dead, you will be saved.'

Remembering the power of this scripture, we can see

that spiritual powers over a nation can be shifted. As Jesus is declared Lord and His Lordship is agreed upon at the gate, the heart and the hill of a nation, a nation is shifted!

Examples from Scripture

In Ephesians 6:12, Paul writes, 'We wrestle not against flesh and blood but against principalities and powers and rulers of the dark places'.

Dark spiritual forces can be shifted out of a nation and out of the leadership of a nation, as the authority of Jesus is established.

Throughout scripture, we see that it was the spiritual powers directing the nations that caused a shift and change in the nations.

King Manasseh shifted spiritual authority in Israel in 2 Chronicles 33:11-17.

When he was young, he set up pagan shrines throughout the land. He was ultimately overcome by the enemy and taken in chains to Babylon. After he repented, God released him back to Israel and he pulled down the pagan altars and re-established sacrifices to God in the temple and the land, and the people again flourished.

Elijah shifted the governmental authority of Israel from Baal to the Kingdom of Heaven as recorded in 1 Kings 18. Elijah challenged the Prophets of Baal who had authority in the nation because of the rule of Ahab and Jezebel. God answered

Elijah by fire. The people saw this and declared, 'The Lord, He is God!'

Elijah then took the prophets of Baal and slaughtered them, cutting off their heads. The headship, i.e. the ungodly authority, was taken out of the land. It took another generation to rise up and defeat the enemy that had been enthroned in the nation. It was Jehu that eventually rose up to defeat Jezebel, but Elijah's showdown at Mount Carmel was the tipping point. God again established Israel under His Lordship.

God sends His ekklesia to transform communities, cities and nations, bringing them under the Lordship of Jesus. Paul showed us that this is entirely possible.

In New Testament times, Paul shifted the cultural mindsets in much of Asia Minor.

Acts 11:26 records, 'It was at Antioch that the believers were first called Christians'.

Paul challenged the spiritual power in Ephesus until a huge power clash erupted.

It was Paul's preaching, teaching and demonstration of the power of God that shifted a whole city and region.

Acts 19:27

'Of course, I'm not just talking about the loss of public respect for our business. I'm also concerned that the temple of the great goddess Artemis will lose its influence and that Artemis—this magnificent goddess worshiped throughout the province of Asia and all around the world—will be robbed of her great prestige!'

Paul's preaching of the Word challenged mindsets and Jewish authorities all over Asia Minor. Believers in the early church went on to transform the culture of Greece. By the third century, the temples of the gods and goddesses of Greece had become churches and they were added to with many new churches peppering the landscape. It is still visible in the ruins today.

Proverbs 29:2

'When the righteous are in authority and become great, the people rejoice; But when the wicked man rules, the people groan and sigh'.

When the righteous rule the people rejoice.

Proverbs 4:18 (AMP)

'The way of the righteous is like the first gleam of dawn, which shines ever brighter until the full light of day.'

This is why God in Deuteronomy 28 urged the people to follow His ways and His righteous paths. He called them to 'choose life'. To choose His ways is to choose abundant life. Nations who will bring their governments under the Lordship of heaven will ensure their nations thrive!

This is not just a theory. In practice, there have been many shifts across nations as this prototype to shift nations has been developed in regions and cities and countries.

Australia - How A Nation Was Shifted

In 2015, the Lord began to alert us of the strategic nature of 2017 for Australia.

October 31, 2017 was the 500 year anniversary of the Reformation that shifted the church into a New Era of faith and freedom. It was also the 100 year anniversary of the ANZAC (Australian and New Zealand Army Corp) 'Light Horse Charge' on Beersheba, that after 2000 years, freed the land of Israel from occupation and made a way for the nation of Israel to be re-established in their land.

These two events in church and world history were monumental. They shaped the world and church we live in today and fulfilled Bible prophecy concerning Israel.

November 11 is 'Remembrance Day'. It was a day of victory for the allies when a treaty was signed in the Pacific declaring WW2 was over and that the allied forces had won. It is a day we remember those who gave their lives for our freedom.

It is 12 days from 31st October to 11th November. The number '12' is the number of government. [13]

The Lord encouraged us (our house of prayer) to commemorate these significant events that established governmental shifts and reformed nations and use this anniversary to again make a shift over Australia.

I sensed Him saying:

Take these 12 days and make a 'governmental shift' over Australia, enthroning Jesus as Lord and shifting the government of God over the nation.

He spoke of having a three hour 'worship watch' at strategic locations, criss-crossing the nation.

Upon praying this through, we understood that we were to go to 12 strategic locations in these twelve days. We were to go to significant gates, to the heart of Australia, Uluru and the hill of government, our national capitol in Canberra.

The catch cry was:

'12 Locations in 12 Days for 1 Shift'.

Awaken the Worshippers, Raise up the Warriors, and Release the Reformers to Shift Australia back under the Government of God.

Our specific strategy:

1. For each of the 12 days we planned a 3 hour worship event that enthroned Jesus at these locations around the nation.
2. These strategic locations were at the Heart, the Gates and the Hill of government of our nation. We believe that Uluru represents the 'heart' of our Nation for both first nation peoples and all other Australians.
3. The 'gate' cities were ten of the twelve strategic locations. These port cities in the nation were locations from where troops had been deployed to both WW1 and WW2. God indicated these ports were to be: Darwin NT., Broome WA., Fremantle (Perth) WA., Albany WA., Adelaide SA., Melbourne Vic., Launceston Tasmania., Sydney NSW, Brisbane Qld and Townsville, Qld.

4. We finished at the 'hill of government' in Canberra on the 11th November: (11.11). (11.11, are key numbers that for us always indicate transition – shift, change, transformation)

5. As much as possible, we united with churches, houses of prayer and indigenous church communities in each city for one united event.

6. We attempted in each location to have believers who were representatives of the first nation's people, representative of the ANZAC, governmental officials and descendants of the Reformation (Protestants) to make decrees at each location.

7. We worshipped and released decrees that:

    - Released the 'government of God' across the nation, enthroning Jesus as Lord over Australia.

    - Released a spirit of reformation and transformation for righteousness and justice to be established in the land.

    - Released the spirit of the ANZACs across the body of Christ, that a new generation would rise in the spirit of the ANZACs and fight for freedom for the people of God (Israel) and the nations.

    - Released unity across the nation, nationalities, denominations, generations and First Nations peoples.

    - Released a spirit of worship and prayer; that Houses of Prayer would increase across our nation and the Army of God would arise to advance the Kingdom of God.

- Raised up the hidden First People's communities and opened a way for the indigenous church to be 'heard' in the nation.

It is estimated we had approximately 300 worshippers across the nation join us at each of these strategic locations. Within those 12 days, we also had other houses of prayer hosting similar three-hour worship events.

It was important to criss-cross the nation in worship, extending the cross of Christ over the land as we went from location to location.

Results

The result was a victory for the Australian houses of prayer and prayer warriors all across the nation and down the generations.

Time and again, as we have conducted major prayer events in different nations, we have seen that God has been orchestrating strategic prayer assignments for that nation. We discover many houses of prayer and prayer warriors that have advanced the Kingdom of God in that nation and have made a way for what we are called to do. Afterward, we have seen how our advance made a way for another prayer strike in the nation that advanced the Kingdom of God even further.

In 2017, the prayer strike around Australia was no different. We saw the Lord mobilize many specific prayer initiatives from prayer houses across the nation and out of Israel. As we reflected on what happened in the nation, we saw how one prayer initiative made way for the next and the next and so on.

We watched the Lord orchestrate this strategic advance across the nation especially throughout the year of 2017.

Different sections of the 'army' of God in the nation were deployed. Each had their own 'strategic assignment' that appeared to make way for the next section of the army to push forward with their assignment.

Many prayers had been prayed by many warriors that brought us to this opportune time to 'shift' a nation! Each one added to the bowls of heaven that brought them closer to being tipped.

Like any battle, there were many fronts. Different troops, groups and houses of prayer around the nation had strategic events that year. Many were on the frontlines in Israel, yet still part of the strategic happenings in Australia.

As each took responsibility for their appointed assignment, ground was being taken in the spirit. Led by the Commander of the Hosts of Heaven's armies, each troop did their part, and we watched as God orchestrate a mighty thrust forward.

We had to wait to see our results. However, 285 days from the end of the Shift the Nation prayer event, Scott Morrison was elected as Australia's first Pentecostal Christian Prime Minister. We understood that 280-285 days is the time of gestation for a human embryo to reach full term. A 'seed' was planted in the nation during those 12 days. It came to full term and was released in the nation in the form of a new leader, unexpectedly thrust into office, 285 days after the prayer event.

Australia now has a righteous leader in office!

A victory was won! Australia has been shifted and now the army of God in Australia continues, through many 'prayer strikes', to continue to advance the Kingdom of God in the nation!

CHAPTER 12

Prayer Strikes

It is our privilege to hear from heaven and receive strategy from the Captain of the Hosts of Heaven's armies. Jesus, as Commander in Chief, is the one who releases strategic insight on how to advance His Kingdom.

Within the framework of the House of Prayer, led by a company of Watchmen Prophets, Priests, Worshippers and Warriors, we receive direction for specific assignments into areas to pull down, break up, build and repair, all that the enemy has stolen.

These assignments into different territories and nations have become known as 'prayer strikes'.

How To Prepare And Mobilize For Prayer Strikes

Prayer to shift cities, territories and nations is not taken lightly.

There are protocols in the spiritual realm that are important to follow. No troop, army or air force engages in military operations against the enemy without being well prepared and adhering to protocol.

There are a number of guidelines that are important to follow.

1. Each prayer strike for a region, city, or nation must be at the direct encouragement of the Lord. It should come with confirmation from other leaders to whom you are accountable. There should also be confirmation from apostolic leaders in the nation to which God is directing.

2. James Goll says, 'You must enter nations under those with apostolic authority in that nation.' This gives protection to you and your team. Many people have suffered a great deal by not using the proper protocol for going into nations.

3. It is helpful to connect with leaders from houses of prayer in the nation to understand the spiritual landscape of the nation.

4. It is important to understand as far as possible what previous prayer strategies have been employed and what the spiritual climate of the nation is. This ensures that these prayers build on prayers of past assignments in the nation.

5. It is essential that the strike be carried out in God's timing. As we have already mentioned, God is a God of timing and order. Nothing is done haphazardly. There is a

time and season for everything. In order to be effective in any assignment, the correct timing is essential. Again, we see this throughout scripture. As God's people move in His timing, there is victory! [1]

6. Most prayer assignments will take some time to prepare. At least six months to twelve months is usually necessary. Prayer and fasting are essential to the preparation and success of the prayer strike. Preparation will involve regular prayer meetings to firstly understand the why, when, and how of the prayer strike itself. Time in prayer for the territory and nation is necessary.

7. During this time, expect dreams, visions and insight. This will often lead to more research and study to uncover historical and geographical information necessary for the prayer strike. It is important to find out the inheritance and spiritual destiny of the location or nation. It is helpful to pray for the leadership of the nation, the spiritual climate in the nation and to understand the nation's policy regarding Israel.

8. Through the process of prayer, God's heart for the nation and the people of the nation is understood.

9. It is also important that we pray with a heart of love and compassion toward the people group or nation to which we are called.

10. Where possible, ask key prayer warriors already in the nation to join you in prayer. Those who live in the nation have authority in the nation. God will connect you with

strategic apostolic prayer leaders. It is also important to connect with First Nations people in the nation. The First Nations people have authority over the land. Their agreement is vital because of the authority they possess.

11. No prayer strike stands alone.

    Every prayer strike stands on the shoulders of the prayer warriors across the nations and down the generations! This army on its knees has heard the voice of the Holy Spirit and followed in prayer to advance the Kingdom in this nation.

    As such, it is necessary to go with the right timing and strategy to ensure the victory of the mission, as often there will be other prayer forces sent in after, to continue the advance.

12. No prayer strike is taken lightly.

    It is a strategic and significant thing to shift ruling powers over any situation. However, God calls us to believe and to enforce what we are believing in prayer.

    Dependency on the leading of the Holy Spirit is vital. *'Not by might or power but by the Spirit of God'* must be the standard. [2]

Weapons That Shift Nations

God's promise is that He will continue to release revelation and authority to equip His army to disciple the nations. Therefore, there is no exhaustive list of weapons of warfare.

However, the list below are the weapons that have been powerfully used to date to shift nations.

1. Power of Specific Strategy

A good strategy is vital in winning any battle. No army goes to war without a strategy that they believe will ensure them victory. Scripture outlines many strategies that God revealed to Israel over many years to secure victory against the enemy.

God's strategies, however, were not always the strategies that a military commander might use. Moses, Joshua, Gideon, Deborah, David and many others throughout the Bible sought the Lord before they went into battle. Each were given specific instructions on how to win the battle; however, all were very different, unconventional and required a leap of faith!

In every battle situation, God has a targeted plan of how to overcome the enemy. It is imperative that we hear from God before we seek to overcome any enemy that is before us. This is true individually and corporately. Even Jesus had to understand the battle plan by meditating through scripture and hearing the voice of God. Jesus was hoping the battle plan could be altered, however, He submitted to it as the Father indicated this was the only way. Jesus would not have overcome the enemy if He had decided that the battle plan the Father gave Him was too hard and He would try a different way!

When God called Gideon in Judges 6, we see a whole process that he went through to ensure he got the victory. Throughout this process we see how God was very patient with him.

1) Firstly, it was necessary for him to hear the call from God and receive the angel that brought the message in the right way. He was righteous in his dealings, which is the foundation for success.

2) Gideon was humble. He did not try to bring any of his own good ideas to this battle. He knew he needed the strategy and power of God to defeat the enemy.

3) He was obedient, even when he was asked to do something difficult. The whole town came out against him, but the Lord kept him safe.

4) He pulled down the idols of his clan and acknowledged God was the Lord. This is essential to have victory in any battle. If there are any idols that we are bowing to, we will not get victory over the enemy. [3]

5) Gideon received and adhered to the specific instruction of the Lord as he went into the battle. God outlines the rules of engagement for His warriors. God looks for men to stand 'in the gap' for Him; that is his first preference. If no-one is found, He will rise up himself, but He prefers to work with His people on the earth. [4]

6) Gideon fought the battle in conjunction with the Lord of the Hosts of Heaven's armies and under His direction. He heard the first instruction but continued to listen to the direction of the Lord. He did not assume the next step. Gideon called the warriors, but God did not want to use all of them. Gideon had to be listening and working with the Lord to ensure that he used the whole strategy of the Lord. God

continues to unfold His strategy as the battle continues. His warriors must be aware of this and continually listen to the Holy Spirit's direction.

7) God fought for Gideon and as he obeyed, there was a sure victory. God, who is the God of all encouragement, encouraged Gideon throughout the battle and God will do the same for all who step out at His call and direction.

It is our great privilege to search out the strategies of Heaven to enforce God's victory in the earth!

2. Enthroning Jesus over Nations

Enthroning Jesus as Lord in any situation gives the Kingdom of Heaven authority in that place. Jesus takes His rightful place as ruler and Lord when a way is made, and He is invited to take His throne in that place.

As explained, to establish Jesus as Lord of our individual lives, we do as Luke 9:10 suggests. We agree at our individual gate, (mouth that makes declaration) heart and hill, (mind) that Jesus is Lord, bringing us into the Kingdom of God.

To achieve the results anticipated for any prayer strike involving strategically going to the gate, the heart and the hill, it was necessary to establish agreement at all three places by enthroning Jesus through praise and worship in these places. There may also be other strategic places God highlights. In Australia, we established this agreement in 10 strategic 'gate' locations as well as the heart and the hill of the nation.

We understood that we were not there to fight principalities and powers and other demonically driven forces that may have taken up residence. Instead, we were there to enthrone Jesus! We were directed to enthrone Jesus in three hours of worship and declaration at each location. As we had agreement of Jesus' Lordship in each of these strategic places, we saw that the principalities and powers over the land could not stand in the Lord's presence. When those in authority agree and enthrone Jesus at the gate, heart and hill of any individual, group or locality, the Lordship of Christ is established. [5]

As Jesus is enthroned, God does the fighting for us. 2 Chronicles 20 is one of the many powerful demonstrations in the Word where God fights for His people. The specific instruction of the Lord was to send the worshippers before the army and give God praise for who He is. This is one of the many premises in scripture for going into battle with worship that enthrones Jesus as our main weapon.

Jehoshaphat was instructed to march the army of Israel to Tekoa and place worshippers in front, praising the Lord as they marched. Tekoa was a gateway into the land. There was a watchtower positioned in that place. [6] It was and still is a high place above the valley that looks out to the direction that the enemy was approaching from. This was a strategic move to enthrone the Lord at the gates of Israel, forbidding the enemy entrance and releasing the power of the Hosts of Heaven's armies against the enemies of God.

God instructed Gideon to release the sound of the trumpeters and set the worshippers at the head of the army. [7] Gideon and his warriors released the sound of the ram's horns and made sounds of smashing pots and released light. This caused the enemy to fight themselves. (8).

In another instance, Moses enthroned Jesus as Lord at the gateway to the Red sea by holding up his staff. God made a way for His people, and the Egyptian Army was defeated without Israel fighting! (9)

All these accounts give proof that when God is for us, and we fight with His heart and strategy, He will fight for us and then the impossible becomes possible.

3. Worship and High Praise to Shifts Nations

Psalms 149:6-9 says,

'Let the exaltation of God be in their mouths and a double-edged sword in their hands, inflicting vengeance on the nations and punishment on the peoples, binding their kings with chains and their dignitaries with iron shackles, carrying out the judgment decreed against them. This honour is for all His godly people. Hallelujah!'

The high praises of God are a militant praise. They are praises that cause the word of the Lord to be activated as weapons with both sound and movement.

Declared in faith, praises and declarations of the Lordship of Christ cause a shift of power. As Jesus is enthroned, it can cause people, people groups and territories to be stripped of unrighteous power.

It can cause the ruling power of a land to be bound and

dethroned so that their power is no longer operating over the nation. God is making judgements against the powers of the enemy, to bring them down and release the people out of their bondage. God is setting peoples free and nations free through the high praises of His people.

While in preparation for a prayer strike,

I saw in the Spirit, God seated on his throne and as the high praises went up to heaven, I saw the throne rise and begin to move. I heard the scripture, 'God inhabits the praise of his people, God is enthroned on the praises of his people'. [10]

As we praised, we perceived that the high praises and worship of the people of God in the earth at strategic locations was shifting the throne of God into our midst. As we raise high praises, His power and presence, at our declarations, will bind the enemy and shift the government of God in our sphere of influence. It is true on an individual level, on a family level, on a corporate level and certainly on a national level.

This is a privilege of the saints, to enthrone Jesus and make declarations in the authority He has given to us. The Lord is causing us to acknowledge the power and authority that we have in our mouths. It is time for the warriors of God to rise and use the authority and weapons we have been given!

Psalms 149:6-9:

'God's high and holy praises fill their mouths,

for their shouted praises are their weapons of war!

'These warring weapons will bring vengeance
on every opposing force and every resistant power—
to bind kings with chains and rulers with iron shackles.

'Praise-filled warriors will enforce the judgment-doom decreed against their enemies.

'This is the glorious honor he gives to all his godly lovers. Hallelujah! Praise the Lord!'

God is a Man of war and He fights with praises, sound, movement and decrees over the power of the enemy. There are new songs, a high praise, singing, dancing, movement and sound that when released, enforces Jesus' victory over the power of the enemy.

Church Pierce released this prophetic word, confirming what I had begun to see. [11]

The Greater the Exultation, the greater the transformation!

I am gathering a people in this hour to exult me like I have never been exalted before.

And if you will exalt me like never before, It will break through realms, it will break through systems, structures, gates, ancient gates that have been in place.

And even in those situations, where the doctor has said one thing, if you will exalt me, like you have never exalted me before, you will see Christ, you will behold me and Christ will be formed within you, Christ will be formed in you in an unprecedented way .

So exalt me in this hour, like you have never exalted me before

I have gathered my people in this hour to put me on display

This is the hour of exultation; this is the hour of transformation within you!

In preparation for these prayer strikes, the Lord has encouraged us to take up new levels of worship that enthrone Him. It is worship that exalts Him and enthrones Him as Lord and lifts Him high over all the power of the enemy.

It is different than soaking worship and worship that declares His love and faithfulness, although both have an essential part in our relationship with the Lord. This worship enthrones Him as Kings of Kings and Lord of Lords. It is worship that declares who He is, declaring His names and therefore the authority of God. It is worship that declares Him as the great I AM.

Chuck Pierce's prophetic word is a call to exalt Jesus. Exult Him with great praise and worship. Exult means 'to lift up.' We were encouraged to lift up Jesus over every aspect and situation for ourselves and the prayer strike. As we enthrone Him, His authority is lifted over every situation and circumstance, all that we say and do becomes subject to His Lordship. When His authority is over our lives, when our lives are shifted into alignment with His authority, then transformation will indeed occur in us and all around us.

There was also an encouragement from heaven, not just to

use this style of worship in warfare, but to have it as part of our lifestyle. Jesus has been directing us to exult Him, with great praise and worship daily.

There are many Houses of Prayer across nations that have been called to raise up the Tabernacle of David again. I believe this is on the heart of the Father, for it is effective in making a way for the establishing of His Kingdom on earth!

4. The Decreed 'Word of the Lord'

As Jesus was enthroned in high praise, the Holy Spirit who is our helper and whom without we can do nothing, released scriptures and gave understanding of what needed to be declared over the situation. These decrees were powerful in their release and we sensed atmospheres shifted as we established Jesus' throne in each place.

We are currently in the Jewish decade of the 80s, equivalent to the Roman calendar of the 20's. In the Hebraic understanding it is the decade of 'Pey', the mouth. The Lord is highlighting the power of the spoken word. In Cambodia, we saw the power of the prophetic decree.

Proverbs 18:20-21
'A man's stomach will be satisfied with the fruit of his mouth;
'He will be satisfied with the consequence of his words.
Death and life are in the power of the tongue,
'And those who love it and indulge it will eat its fruit and bear the consequences of their words'.

The release of the prophetic word from the heart of God through His people has the power of life and death. As the people of God speak the prophetic word from the Spirit, it becomes a powerful 'now' word of resurrection life to individuals, families and nations. Words decreed in faith, in the power of an unbroken covenant and direction of the Holy Spirit have the power to shift and transform! In meditating and storing up the word of God, it can be released as powerful seeds that can produce abundant life.

5. The Power of Prophetic Acts

The prophets of both the Old and New Testament powerfully used prophetic actions to illustrate in the natural what God was enforcing in the spirit realm.

In scripture, Elisha was lying sick on his bed, in his own home, knowing he was about to die. The king had come to visit, and Elisha instructed him to do a prophetic act. He asked the King to shoot an arrow from the window toward the nation of Aram, the nation that was currently oppressing Israel. [12] He then declared that Israel would conquer that nation.

Elisha also instructed the King to strike the arrows he still had on the ground. He only struck the arrows three times. Elisha was hoping he would have done it more. Three strikes on the ground only meant partial victory. [13]

Amazingly, this prophetic act and the declaration that followed from Elisha, set the course of a nation's future. It seems remarkable that a prophetic act from a dying man's bedroom could change the course of a nation, yet it did.

The prophetic act is very powerful and although at times seemingly mundane and innocent, we cannot neglect to follow through, for in faith it brings heaven's will to pass on earth!

In the New Testament, Jesus is coming into Jerusalem. The crowds hail Him as King and receive Him into the earth as the King. This was a prophetic act and declaration that acknowledged that the King of Heaven had come to take up His authority over the heavens and the earth! It displayed God's will on earth and shifted the heavens to enforce this victory of God's will! It is one of only a handful of prophetic acts of Jesus that is recorded in all four gospels. (14)

When God's will is outplayed prophetically through action in the physical realm, it has the authority of the spoken decree. Job 28:22 states, *'Decree a thing and it will happen!'* Scripture abounds, especially throughout the Old Testament, with prophetic acts in the natural that symbolize and activate God's will. It declares to the spiritual realms and authorities God's purposes and makes a way for God's will to be established on the earth.

6. The Power of the Prayer of Agreement

Agreement on earth between believers dispels darkness and wins battles in the heavens where other things cannot.

Matthew 18:18-19

'Receive this truth: Whatever you forbid on earth will be considered to be forbidden in heaven, and whatever you release on earth will be considered to be released in heaven. Again, I give you an eternal truth: If two of you agree to ask God for something in a symphony of prayer, my heavenly Father will do it for you'.

Agreement between believers on earth releases exponential power in the spiritual realm. Agreement on the earth has the power to shift atmospheres and push back an enemy that as individuals we are incapable of defeating. The use of the power of agreement is vital to the church of Jesus Christ. As an army that is called to defeat the enemy and evict him from territories, this weapon is vital.

Genesis 6 tells the story of the Tower of Babel. In oneness they could achieve anything. This is a great encouragement. Jesus' prayer that it be 'on earth as it is in heaven' is suddenly possible, when the people of God are unified.

Psalm 68 declares,

'One can put one thousand to flight and two can put ten thousand to flight'.

This scripture suggests that the greater the number who agree together, the greater the power to push back the enemy. The enemy is aware of this truth and has powerful assignments of disunity and discord that he sends against the people of God. It is His purpose to keep the body of Christ in disunity.

Unity, however, cannot be strived for by human effort. In fact, in the effort of striving and then failing, many have been discouraged and given up in defeat.

Oneness of the Spirit is achieved through the increase of the knowledge of the Lord and His glory in our midst. [15] Agreement of our natural minds on anything is very difficult to achieve. However, as we pursue the knowledge of who Jesus is and His presence in our midst, the glory will draw the believers together as one with Jesus. When glory realms are opened, more is wrought in the glory presence than we know. The glory within can be a reality.

Zechariah 2:5

'He will be a wall of fire around and he will be the glory within.'

In this New Era of glory, God is increasing His glory around His people so that we can be released in oneness.

Oneness is also achieved when a common enemy is recognised. Even people that are not friends will come together to fight against a common foe. We see the example in scripture when both Pilot and Herod were involved in Jesus trial.

When the true enemy of our souls is clearly recognised, the army will come together in unity against our common foe, the devil. [16]

7. Coming in the Opposite Spirit

Coming in an opposite spirit is an effective tool of warfare individually and corporately. The Apostle Paul encourages us to be like Jesus and overcome evil with good. [17]

Jesus said to 'Love your enemies, do good to those who hate

you, bless those who curse you.' (18) As we do this, we activate the power of the Holy Spirit in a situation and often we see the situation turn around. Again, this can be done individually and even on a national level.

When Jesus fed the 5000, he broke many old mindsets in the people, least of all, poverty, stinginess, and greed. It happened through a little boy who was able to come in the opposite spirit and sacrifice his own food to feed others. Coming in the opposite spirit can shift mindsets and release truth to those bound.

Indonesia was devastated by a tsunami in 1994. At the time, Australia's relationship with Indonesia had been strained. The government of Australia responded immediately with aid and resources. Upon realizing the enormity of the devastation, the then Prime Minister pledged one billion dollars in aid over the following ten years. It was an outrageously generous amount. Many nations pledged funds and were also very generous, but this was above and beyond.

Immediately, the ties between Australia and Indonesia were repaired and remained that way for many years. Interestingly, Australia was able to weather the Global Financial Crisis of 2008, that seriously impacted many other economies.

When you come in an opposite spirit, it gives power to the Holy Spirit in the situation and you reap the blessing for sowing to the Spirit.

Hosea 10:12

'I said, 'Plant the good seeds of righteousness,

and you will harvest a crop of love'.

As we pray for nations, as with individuals, we can come in the opposite spirit.

While praying at the large temple at 'Angkor Wat' in Cambodia, we could have been very intimidated; however the strategy of the Lord was to come in the opposite spirit.

Instead of standing against the huge spirit of deception, death, depravity, and decimation represented by this structure, we were directed to celebrate.

Coming in an opposite spirit, with about 20 people, we sat down as if we were picnicking. We played guitars and sang and danced. We celebrated before the Lord and feasted in the presence of our enemies. Along with many other prophetic acts, we decreed that the heart of Cambodia was now captured by Jesus and Cambodia could become a nation of His inheritance.

Weapons Of Increased Revelation And Authority

Recently, when spending time with God, I saw myself taken up to the heavenly realm.

I was sitting at a long white table - like a wedding table, it had a white skirt.

There was a group of about eight of ten of us and we were discussing strategies for how to take the Kingdom into nations on the earth.

We had all our blueprints out on the table, and we were

looking out over the table onto the earth as we discussed the nations.

Suddenly a huge angel flew up in front of us with a mighty whoosh!

I knew immediately that it was Michael.

He stood a little side on and then with a huge swipe of his hands He swiped everything off the table. He indicated these plans were obsolete and then he said to us and also indicated and to other angels who had then amassed around us,

'The Lord has a storehouse of new weapons stored and kept for this time'.

He indicated to the angels to go and open the store house, for we had come to the appointed time!

As we waited, it seemed like there were two major weapons that were about to come forth.

They were new weapons that we had not used before. The angle declared that the new weapons were:

1. Increased Revelation

2. Greater Authority.

Let's seek Him in His glory realm for greater dimensions of revelation and authority. Greater revelation knowledge and insight is the promise of this year 2020. Without continued revelation the bible says the people perish. As such, greater vision will bring the opportunity to flourish. With the promise of greater authority also comes the promise of greater ability to shift the Kingdom of Heaven by the revelation knowledge released to us.

With increased revelation and greater authority, the people of God can rise and shine, living as overcomers and taking territory for the Kingdom of God in the earth.

This Is The Moment

There is a song, sung by Anthony Warlow entitled, 'This is the Moment'!

I believe that God is announcing that indeed, 'this is the moment, this is the time'!

God himself has stepped into time to effect change and shift on the earth through His presence and His power. This is HIS moment and HIS time!

I believe this to be one of God's great moments in world history.

In Noah's time, in Abraham's time, in Moses' time, in Jesus' time, God Himself stepped into the world's history to show Himself as God, the God who rules the nations and shows Himself strong on behalf of His people.

We are in a series of moments of moments.

Just as the Israelites, the people of God, were brought out of Egypt in a series of spectacular victories over the world powers, God is releasing His people, in the same way.

We will have an opportunity to rise up and step out of the old bondages and familiar patterns of life and see remarkable shift and change into a whole new operating system and lifestyle of the Spirit.

God Himself will go before us to release us with signs, wonders and miracles from His hand! As with the children of Israel, it will not be without struggle, but as with the children of Israel, we will stand in AWE of our God!

Again, through a series of spectacular divine moments, Joshua led the people of Israel out of the wilderness and into the promised land. The world around them saw the power of God and His favour to His people. I believe that we are in the season where God is doing it again.

There will be a series of remarkable events, a series of momentous moments in our lives and in world history, where we will have opportunity to grab hold of God and shift with Him out of old bondage and restrictions and into freedom and newness of life!

The Son has been wooing His Bride and now as Lord, Jesus is empowering His bride, with the 'spirit of the power of might'.

In the spirit, I have seen the Lord, as the Warrior Bridegroom, with the Host of Heaven's armies, come to His bride, put the finishing touches to her veil and lift her by His grace into His chariot to ride into battle with Him. [19]

I saw the same spirit that was on Samson come upon the bride, and her veil begin to grow, just like Samson's hair grew. As she stepped out, the chains that had her bound, snapped just like the new ropes that had Samson bound.[20] Like Samson, the bride easily broke out of the restrictions and was free from the enemy's plan.

The Lord is endowing His people with the spirit of might, that same spirit that was upon Samson (Isaiah11:2). The weapons that the enemy has used to contain us and keep us bound, God is now releasing new power and authority to break.

It's time again to rise against the enemies of the past that we have been unable to be throw off, for they are now being supernaturally broken off as the spirit of might and the spirit power is increasing in His bride.

Through the knowledge of His love, He is empowering His bride to rise above all fear and grip of the enemy. Song of Solomon 7:1-8 (TPT)

> Even a King is held captive by your beauty!
> You stand in victory above the rest, stately and secure,
> as you share with me your vineyard of love.
> Now I decree, 'I will ascend and arise. I will take hold of you with my power, possessing every part of my fruitful bride.'

This grace is among us for deliverance, breakthrough and shift from the world system, to abundant life. It is a complete change, a shift into living with the new heart and the new mind that He has put within us.

It is a shift into living as His righteous people in the land, possessing all the benefits of righteousness.

It is a step up to believe and see the great and precious promises He has for us materialise in a great harvest of loved ones saved, relationships mended, love poured out between the generations, long standing sickness healed, infirmity eradicated, disease obliterated and lives restored.

It is time to move on forward into our victory and life in the promised land!

'This is the Moment'
by Frank Wildhorn and Leslie Bricusse

This is the moment! This is the day,
When I send all my doubts and demons on their way!
Every endeavour, I have made –ever–
Is coming into play, is here and now – today!

This is the moment, This is the time,
When the momentum and the moment are in rhyme!
Give me this moment – This precious chance -
I'll gather up my past And make some sense at last!

This is the moment, when all I've done -
All the dreaming, scheming and screaming, become one!
This is the day, See it sparkle and shine,
When all I've lived for Becomes mine!

This is the moment - My final test -
Destiny beckons I never reckoned, Second Best!

I won't look down, I must not fall!
This is the moment, The sweetest moment of them all!

This is the moment! Forget all the odds!
This day and ever, I'll sit forever, With My God!
When I look back, I will always recall,
Moment for moment, This was the moment,
The greatest moment Of them all! [21]

I believe we will look back at this time and realise that we were in one of the greatest moments in world history, for the body of Christ and the advancing of the Kingdom of God on earth.

CHAPTER 13

Commissioned into a Movement

This Moment Is Now To Become A Movement!

In September 2014, I had a vision that confirmed to me what I suspected. God is calling up a new company of champions assigned to advance His Kingdom in a New Era.

I saw a band of troops coming across the coastline. Their shields of faith where held high over their heads and locked together. The sun reflecting off these shields made the army look like a golden river flooding over the land. As they moved forward, they fanned out in separate tributaries and ran like rivers across my nation of Australia. I knew that this was the army of God prepared, called and moving forward as one. They moved across the nation to make way to establish the Kingdom of God in the land.

I believe that God is calling up His troops. He is calling not just a company, but a movement of His overcoming warriors to advance His Kingdom. A new glory rests upon this people of God and the oneness between them is producing a movement that cannot be stopped.

I believe God is raising up a movement of champion warriors, flowing in many streams, across nations. It is His end time army of overcomers. They are warriors of 'resurrection life', who will 'make way for the Lord of the Harvest', to gather the great harvest of the nations. As these warriors of God move forward in overcoming prayer, with the shield of faith raised, the prayer of faith will release the power and presence of the Kingdom to reap billions in the nations as has been prophesied.

Lou Engle quotes, 'Every great move of God is preceded by a great move of prayer.' The prophets have been declaring a great harvest is now at hand. As such, a great move of prayer is at hand, and has in part already begun.

This movement will gain momentum as the revelation comes to the people of God that everyone in the body of Christ is a warrior. As each one is called to be a warrior and trained to dispel the darkness and release the light of Christ, the body of Christ will rise with authority to disciple the nations. That's the privilege of the army of the Lord.

I am not of course, speaking of warriors in the natural, I am speaking of those 'who wrestle not against flesh and blood but against principalities and powers in the heavenly realms'. The weapons we use are not natural, but they are mighty through

God for the pulling down of strongholds. These weapons of our warfare are activated by prayer. [1]

It is the passion and privilege of all who pursue God and the advancing of His Kingdom to meet heaven in prayer. The ekklesia of God can facilitate the release of heaven's real answers into the earth as they first connect with heaven, then release heaven's strategy on earth to empower the nation for change.

The spiritual war in this age across the nations of the earth is getting more and more intense. Many once comfortable Christian nations in which the gospel was accepted and promoted are now fighting to maintain their Christian heritage.

God is again calling and equipping His church to rise and impact the state of society and the lifestyle of people and people groups as Christ intended. Understanding the power of prayer and rising up to pray is vital to the church demonstrating and releasing the Kingdom of Heaven as the answer for the nations.

God is calling for a movement of His prayer warriors all across the earth to divinely shift and disciple the nations of the earth, preparing Jesus' inheritance in the earth!

As the ekklesia of God, the church of Jesus Christ is in the connection between Heaven and earth. We have a power and authority that we do not yet fully understand.

Examine the moon. The moon is a prophetic picture of the bride of Christ, the church. [2]

We only see the moon because it picks up the light of the sun and shines it into the earth. It waxes and wanes at its positioning before the sun. When totally aligned, it gives the full reflection of the sun. However, even when partially aligned, its brightness and beauty and light are still visible.

The people of God are no different; we reflect the light of Christ in the earth and we influence the earth to the extent that we are rightly aligned with Christ.

The pull of the moon upon the earth influences the seas and oceans of the world. The tides go in and out at the movement of the moon around the earth.

Likewise. the ocean of humanity is directly influenced by the movement of the people of God upon the earth.

As the people of God move to bring the light of Christ into the darkness of the earth, the sea of humanity will be directly influenced. When the light of Christ is visible, the earth will come out of darkness into light.

There is nothing more beautiful and reflective of the glory of God upon the earth than the moon reflecting upon the ocean. As the people of God shine the light of God on earth, the glory of God will be poured out on the ocean of humanity. When God's glory, that is His goodness, is seen in the earth, the people will understand the love and kindness of the Lord.

At times, regardless of its positioning before the sun, the moon can be hidden by the many differing cloud masses that may limit the earth's ability to see the moon.

At times, the earth itself can totally block the earth's ability to see moon as the earth eclipses the moon.

This however, does not make the moon any less powerful in its ability to affect the movement of the ocean of the earth.

The people of God all across the earth, ruling in their rightful position in the nations, can shift the tide of humanity! Rightly reflecting Jesus and releasing the light of Christ and the glory of the Father into the earth, can shift and change our world!

We Have Lift-Off!

In the midst of the on-going CoVid-19 pandemic, in June 2020, the USA launched a spaceship into space. Remarkable images flashed onto screens everywhere as we watched the launch of the SpaceX Crew Dragon!

This was very exciting to see. It seemed like a demonstration of what God is doing in the spiritual realm.

As this spacecraft launched into a further dimension of space, it seems God is launching His people into the New Era and into greater access of the heavenly dimensions of His glory!

As I listened to the commentary, I heard phases like:

'A New generation continuing the dream!'

We, the generation living now, are the ones that continue the dreams of the Father to see His Kingdom come on earth as it is in heaven!'

The NASA SpaceX launch continued the dream. However, they were using a whole new operating system with new equipment.

1) The space shuttle was new.
   God is giving us a new wineskin. Church will no longer just be meeting in buildings! (Luke 5:37-38)
2) The operating system was new.
   NASA's operating system combined with SpaceX is the good of the old combined with the new.
3) New generation clothing was worn (a new style of spacesuit).
   God is supernaturally placing new mantles upon us that will cause us to operate more freely as we live from heaven to earth.
4) The rocket was operated in a new way.
   The first stage of the rocket was brought back to the earth. This means a more efficient, less expensive operations for future travel. God is giving us inventive ways to operate more efficiently, with less drain on resource. God is upgrading our operating systems.

'All systems are go!'

The menace of CoVid-19 continues to attempt to shut in and shut down people and nations, however, God is launching His church in a whole new way.

It gives the church an opportunity to now launch out into the harvest field in a whole new way. There are great new opportunities to reap the harvest that is full and ready for harvesting. (Matthew 9:37-38)

'Did you hear the 'roar' of the engines!'

The Church of Jesus Christ will no longer be hidden, shut down and silent in the midst of the community. It is a new day where the voice of the people of God in nations will be heard again. As the Lion of Judah roars from heaven to earth, His presence and power will be heard and demonstrated with power!

'The rocket went up at supersonic speed!'

Supersonic speed is beyond the speed of sound. After Stage1 was released, the rocket sped along at 2.3g's of gravitational force, breaking out of the earth's gravitational pull.

The body of Christ should no longer be held down by the forces in the earth. The Lord is releasing us to 'fly' in the heavens with Him. There is a greater release and knowledge of the supernatural dimension for the people of God. The word of prophecy, dreams and visions, heavenly encounters, and even supernatural translations will become common among the people of God.

'Go Bob 'n' Doug!' (These were the names of the men who captained the vessel)

The men leading this launch were fathers, both family men with wives and children.

This New Era in the church will be spearheaded and established by those with a fathering, apostolic anointing. They will understand their critical and foundational position in the family of God. They will have a gracious loving and wise father's anointing to mature the body and bring them into alignment with heaven and one another. The family will flourish under their care as they lay down their lives and lead as foundations upon which the family can build. (Ephesians 4:12)

'Flawless, fantastic launch!'

God has been preparing, perfecting and purifying His people for a new season of His glory pouring out. God is giving His people time in this pandemic world to embrace change and to complete the work He has begun. He is calling us to rise in confidence, shining His nature, passion and power. He is calling His body as righteous and Holy to walk in confidence. As we trust Jesus, He will launch us into the New Era! All that He does is perfect.

'Momentous occasion during this time of the pandemic and riots!'

Yes, it is a momentous occasion to see what God is doing across the body of Christ! However, the enemy is also aware of the huge shift and change that God is supernaturally bringing to the earth. The enemy is throwing everything He can to stop the progression of the Spirit of God upon the earth.

Don't be alarmed at what is happening around us. However, know the shaking is NOT over! The enemy himself is alarmed and is mustering all his forces against the people of God and the nations called to righteousness.

I believe we are in a time like the time of Jesus. The enemy would not have sent Jesus to the Cross had he understood what God would accomplish through His death and resurrection. (1 Corinthians 2:8)

The enemy would not keep releasing the trauma of the pandemic, riots and economic crisis if he knew what God is launching in this time.

'Launch!'

I heard the Lord say that He will launch His people out by His spirit into dimensions of the heavenly realms we have not been before.

We will know Him! and as we do, we will light up where we go!

We will be the light in the darkness and point the way for others.

There will be a quick transformation:

Like the Hulk, we will change in moments.

Like a tree that grows and breaks through the concrete, we will come out of the most intense of restrictions and break through into a whole new world of revival and reformation!

There is an excitement in the Spirit for the new things ahead.

God has launched His people into the New Era, and with it comes great possibilities for the future of people groups and nations.

God has promised to bless His people, that we might be a blessing to all the peoples of the nations.⁽³⁾ God's plan is to have rulership in the nations through His people, to establish righteousness and justice and all the blessings that this brings.

As children who know their God, let's rise as one people and move forward in our authority to shift the nations.

For the sake of a dying world, desperate to know the love and goodness of the Father, let's rise and shine together in the power and love of God.

Let the movement begin! Let the army arise!

End Notes

Chapter 1
1. The Renaissance.
   See https://en.wikipedia.org/wiki/Renaissance
2. Exodus 12:51 – 'On that very day the Lord brought the people of Israel out of the land of Egypt like an army'.
3. Joshua 10:20
4. Luke 2:13-14 – "Glory to God in the highest realms of heaven! For there is peace and a good hope given to the sons of men."
5. 1 Kings 10:6-8
6. https://en.wikipedia.org/wiki/Constantine_the_Great

Chapter 2
1. Benefits of Righteousness
   Psalms 119:142 (TPT) – Your righteousness has no end; it is everlasting, and your rules are perfectly fair.
   Proverbs 11:18 (TPT) – Evil people may get a short-term gain, but to sow seeds of righteousness will bring a true and lasting reward.
   Psalms 99:4 (TPT) – A lover of justice is our mighty King; he is right in all His ways. He insists on being fair to all, promoting true justice and righteousness in Jacob.
2. Justice in the Old Testament.
   Amos 2:4-5 – God's Judgment on Judah and Israel
   This is what the Lord says: "The people of Judah have sinned again and again, and I will not let them go unpunished! They have rejected the instruction of the Lord, refusing to obey His decrees. They have been led astray by the same lies that deceived their ancestors. So I will send down fire on Judah, and all the fortresses of Jerusalem will be destroyed."

3. Justified by the blood of Jesus
   Romans 3:25-26
   ²⁵ For God presented Jesus as the sacrifice for sin. People are made right with God when they believe that Jesus sacrificed His life, shedding His blood. This sacrifice shows that God was being fair when he held back and did not punish those who sinned in times past, ²⁶ for he was looking ahead and including them in what he would do in this present time. God did this to demonstrate His righteousness, for he himself is fair and just, and he makes sinners right in His sight when they believe in Jesus.
4. 2 Peter 3:9
5. Ed Silvoso sites Acts 19:32-41 as an example of the working 'ekklesia' of the Roman Empire.
6. Ekklesia: Rediscovering God's Instrument for Global Transformation. by Ed Silvoso. – Chosen Books ebook edition 2017. Chapter 1.
7. John 18:36
   Jesus looked at Pilate and said, "The royal power of my kingdom realm doesn't come from this world. If it did, then my followers would be fighting to the end to defend me from the Jewish leaders. My kingdom realm authority is not from this realm."
8. James 2:23 (NLT)
9. Isaiah 60:1-2

Chapter 3

1. Christian International
   https://christianinternational.com/blog/2016/7/8/origin-of-7-mountain-concepts-and-7mki?rq=7%20mountains
2. The Reformation Manifesto by Cindy Jacobs.
   Bethany Publishing House. Minneapolis Minnesota 2008. p.15
3. Creating A Supernatural Atmosphere - Conference at GZI 2020. Day 2.
4. a) Saved, salvation.
   Cognate: 4991 sōtēría (from 4982 /sōzō, "to save, rescue")

– salvation, i.e. God's rescue which delivers believers out of destruction and into His safety.
https://biblehub.com/greek/4991.htm
b) Galatians 3:8 (TPT)
5. C. Peter Wagner Dominion: How Kingdom Action Can Change the World. Chosen Books. 2008. Introduction.
6. C. Peter Wagner - Wrestling with Alligators, Prophets and Theologians - Regal from Gospel Light 2010 - p.214
7. https://billygraham.org/story/franklin-graham-launching-50-city-tour-in-2016/
8. https://www.nytimes.com/2019/11/02/us/politics/paula-white-trump.html
9. https://saltandlight.sg/news/lord-i-am-not-asking-for-a-million-dollars-but-for-a-million-souls-the-late-reinhard-bonnke/

Chapter 4
1. Joshua 1:3-9
2. Joshua 2:9-11
"I know the Lord has given you this land," she told them. "We are all afraid of you. Everyone in the land is living in terror."

Chapter 5
1. Exodus 3:1-4 (New Messianic Version Bible)
"Now Moshe [He Who Draws Out Of The Waters] kept the flock of Yitro [Excellence] his father in law, the priest of Midyan [Strife]: and he led the flock to the backside of the desert, and came to the mountain of God-Elōhīm (The Living Word) [The Many Powered], [even] to Horev [Desert]. And the angel of the Lord -Yehōvah (Messiah Pre-Incarnate) appeared unto him in a flame of fire out of the midst of a bush: and he looked, and, behold, the bush burned with fire, and the bush [was] not consumed. And Moshe [He Who Draws Out Of The Waters] said, I will now turn aside, and see this great sight, why the bush is not burnt. And when the Lord -Yehōvah (Messiah

Pre-Incarnate) saw that he turned aside to see, God-Elōhīm [The Living Word] called unto him out of the midst of the bush, and said, Moshe, Moshe [He Who Draws Out Of The Waters]. And he said, Here [am] I.

2. https://lp.israelbiblicalstudies.com/lp_iibs_biblical_hebrew_i_am_who_i_am-en.html?_atscid=3_2483_207646268_9821117_0_Txtdwewxdzshpcwcspdand_at=0.3.9821117,0.207646268.xtdwewxdzshpcwcspdandcid=70175andadgroupid=-1andutm_source=Email_Marketingandutm_medium=I_Am_Who_I_Am_05_19andutm_campaign=BIB_EN_EML_I_Am_Who_I_Am_2019-05-23_70175andcommChannel=1andstid=6844844andhash=630a688d5ebfa2ddabb76e3a8396ca1d
Elohim ("God").
YHWH ("Lord') (Pre-incarnate Messiah)

3. On the top of Horeb, the Mountain of God, Moses comes face-to-face with the Lord and dares to ask his name. God's cryptic response is "I am who I am". This is an odd response because it is not a name but more of a motto. In the original Hebrew, what God actually says is ehiyeh asher ehiyeh. Right away you can hear the similarity between the sound of the word "I am" (ehiyeh) and the holiest name of the Lord (Yahweh). Both words have to do with being.

4. John 8:58

5. Lou Engle, The Jesus Fast, Chosen Books, Minnesota @2016. Introduction.

6. Habakkuk 2:14

7. https://reformationharvestfire.com/2016/03/che-ahn-its-time-for-bob-jones-prophesied-billion-soul-harvest/

8. Revelation 11:15

Chapter 6

1. Bill Hamon - Apostles, Prophets and the Coming Move of God – Destiny Image Publishers (1997) Chapter 1.

2. Ephesians 4:11-12, Ephesians 2:20

END NOTES 271

3. C. Peter Wagner - Apostolic Centers Arising, Traditional Churches and Apostolic Centers, A National Consultation on Apostolic Centers, Glory of Zion Ministries, June 2014
4. 1 Samuel 17:26
5. Revelation 19:13-15

Chapter 7

1. Acts 6:4 – ⁴Then we apostles can spend our time in prayer and teaching the word.
2. Daniel 9
3. Tim Sheets Angel Armies Destiny Image Publishes. 2019 - p.87, 88.
4. Jeff Jansen The Elijah Company: A New Prophetic Eagle Rising – https://www.facebook.com/JeffJansenFanPage/posts/jeff-jansen-elijah-company-rising-in-nations/10155226523146241/
5. Luke 11:25
6. Charlie Shamp: A New Prophetic Bird is being birthed in the Earth. https://www.elijahlist.com/words/display_word.html?ID=18068
7. http://www.freebiblecommentary.org/special_topics/prophet.html Copyright © 2014
8. Jim W. Goll The Seer Destiny Image Publishes, PA, USA. 2004. Ch.1, p.23.
9. ibid p.22
10. http://www.freebiblecommentary.org/special_topics/prophet.html
Copyright © 2014
11. Dr. Chuck D. Pierce, Re-Ordering Your Day Glory of Zion International Ministries. 2006. p.24
12. Jim W. Goll The Seer Destiny Image Publishes, PA, USA. 2004. Ch.1, p.23.
13. Ezekiel 11, 14, 18 show Ezekiel caught in the glory of God and prophesying for the Sovereign Lord.
14. Ezekiel 3:16-19, 33:6

15. Ezekiel 21, 26, 29, 31
16. Ezekiel 2:3
17. Isaiah 62:6
18. Ezekiel 36, 37, 39
19. Habakkuk 2:2
20. Daniel 2:48
21. Charlie Shamp: A New Prophetic Bird is being birthed in the Earth. https://www.elijahlist.com/words/display_word.html?ID=18068
22. Dr. Chuck D. Pierce, Re-Ordering Your Day Glory of Zion International Ministeries. 2006. p.25
23. Chuck Pierce: Call for Watchman Prophets. https://youtu.be/wQKLm6U8YhE
24. 2 Chronicles 29:30
25. Joshua 6:4-5
26. 2 Chronicles 20:22
27. 2 Samuel 6:12-14
28. 1 Chronicles 16:4
29. Luke 2:36-38

Chapter 8
1. Daniel 3:25-27
2. Ezekiel 2:3
3. Ecclesiastes 3:1
4. John 7:30
5. Exodus 13:8-10
6. Joshua 6:12-14, Judges 7:19, Judges 16:3
7. 1 Kings 18:36-37
8. Heflin, Ruth. Glory-Experiencing the Atmosphere of Heaven. McDougal Publishing. Kindle Edition. Copyright © 2012. location 984, 43%

9. 2 Samuel 21
10. Jeremiah 1:8
11. Isaiah 11:11-12
12. Matthew 5:8
13. 1 Peter 2:9
14. John 14:30

PART 2
Chapter 9
1. Matthew 28:19
2. Matthew Henry's Commentary - *https://www.biblestudytools.com/commentaries/matthew-henry-complete/matthew/28.html* - Matthew 28
3. ibid
4. Matthew 6:10
5. Genesis 12:1-3
6. Amos 3:7
7. Genesis 18:16-33
8. Jonah 3:6-10
9. 1 Kings 18:40
10. Isaiah 40:3
11. Isaiah 43:19-21
12. Matthew 3:3
13. Isaiah 21 v.1-10 Babylon, v. 11-12 Edom, v.13-17 Arabia.
14. Daniel 4:27-30
15. Jonah 3:6-9
16. Jonah 3:10
17. Ephesians 1:19-23
18. *https://www.biography.com/political-figure/constantine-i* p.1

19. *https://en.wikipedia.org/wiki/Christianity_in_Europe* Introduction
    https://en.wikipedia.org/wiki/Christian_state page 1
20. *https://www.insider.com/20-most-prosperous-nations-2019-legatum-index-2019-11#10-iceland-11*
21. ibid no.18
22. Isaiah 1
23. Deuteronomy 30:19-20
24. John 10:10
25. Isaiah 40:1b (TPT)

Chapter 10

1. James 3:16
2. Matthew 6:10
3. Ephesians 2:6
4. Hebrews 7:25
5. Acts 13:2-3
6. Matthew 28:18
7. Colossians 1:22
8. Romans 8:1
9. *https://renewaljournal.com/2011/09/12/snapshots-of-glory-bygeorge-otis-jr/* Renewal Journal George Otis Jnr. Almolonga, Guatemala
10. Ezekiel 22:30
11. Psalms 44:3-4
12. 'to fast' is to wage war
13. Robert Heidler, The Triumphant Kingdom: The Apostolic Church Advancing, Published by Glory of Zion International Ministries, Inc. @2019 p. 118
14. https://www.jstor.org/stable/42971881?seq=1
15. https://en.wikipedia.org/wiki/First_Great_Awakening

Chapter 11
1. Isaiah 51:4-5
2. 1 Kings 11:1-3
3. Ruth 4:7-9
4. John 10:7-9
5. Romans 3:25-26
6. Exodus 12:13
7. Joshua 6:20
8. Nehemiah 1:3-4, 4:6
9. Ruth 3:1-12
10. Judges 16:3
11. https://www.smh.com.au/national/act/mateship-courage-and-sacrifice-honoured-at-australian-war-memorial-20180425-p4zbkh.html
12. https://en.wikipedia.org/wiki/Pledge_of_Allegiance
13. https://www.biblestudy.org/bibleref/meaning-of-numbers-in-bible/12.html

Chapter 12
1. Joshua 1:2
2. Zechariah 4:6
3. Judges 6:25-26
4. Isaiah 59:16
5. 1 Corinthians 7:14
6. 2 Chronicles 20:24
7. Joshua 6:8-11
8. Judges 6:21
9. Exodus 14:21-28
10. Psalms 22:3
11. Chuck Pierce, Glory of Zion. Prophetic Word, 31.1.2016

12. 2 Kings 13:14-17
13. 2 Kings 13:18-19
14. Matthew 21:1, Mark 11:1, Luke 19:28, John 12:12
15. Ephesians 1:3-4
16. Luke 23:12
17. Romans 12:21
18. Luke 6:27
19. Song of Songs 3:10
20. Judges 16:1-8
21. https://www.youtube.com/watch?v=9KiX2Wgo7hg
    This is the Moment by Frank Wildhorn and Leslie Bricusse (modified for our purposes, with apologies to the song writers)

Chapter 13

1. 2 Corinthians 10:4
2. Genesis 37:9
   The Sun and the moon featured in Joseph's famous dream, was interpreted by Jacob to be referring to his wife, the mother of Joseph. The moon being likened to a wife, suggests that the moon can be a picture of a wife, even the bride of Christ, the church.
3. Genesis 12:12

Appendix

Appendix 1

Charlie Shamp's Full Prophetic Word

A New Prophetic Mantle of Three

The Lord spoke to me and said that He is stitching together a prophetic mantle, reserved in Heaven, for the new company of prophets He wants to release on the earth. He called them the Bridal company. This garment is being stitched together by a three-cord strand through the spirit of unity and bonded together through the bond of peace.

I heard the Lord say, "I am gathering from three different prophetic movements that I have birthed in the earth from the past. These were three distinct, heavenly birds that I sent to the earth, and they built prophetic nests for me. They have come home to Heaven, but they multiplied themselves and released their mantles upon their children before they left the earth.

"I will pull at their sons and daughters heart strings in this season with a new prophetic sound in an attempt to knit them together so their movements will fly as one. This will happen if they hear the new sound and catch the fresh wind that is about to come. When this happens, I will release a new prophetic movement—a new bird will come."

The Bridal Company—A Threefold Cord

I then saw in the spirit a mantle come out of Heaven carried by the wind of His Word. Engraved on this mantle was the phrase, "A threefold cord is not easily broken" (Ecclesiastes 4:12). Then I was shown the other side of the mantle. Engraved on this side were the words, "Behold, they are written in the book of Samuel the seer, and in the book of Nathan the prophet, and in the book of Gad the seer" (1 Chronicles 29:29).

I again heard the Lord say, "I am offering to the sons of the prophets the same mantle that I gave Elisha, a heavenly legacy. This is a double portion of the prophetic and is the inheritance only given to the first born, but I will lay it upon those who catch this new wind that I am releasing from My throne. They will receive it and fly together in the unity of the Spirit."

Suddenly, I saw a mighty, rushing wind released from the throne room, and it blew across the earth. I saw three different birds take flight simultaneously and soar together as one.

The Golden Eagle

The golden eagle represented the seer prophets. Those who are given supernatural insights and heavenly revelation through dreams and visions. They carry a wonder-working power of the supernatural. They often manifest unusual wonders and manifestations of the glory.

The Silver Winged Dove

The silver winged dove represented the nabi prophets. Those that spontaneously prophesy as the Spirit moves upon them. They are given a ministry of signs that manifest in the area of deliverance and healing.

The Snow White Owl

The snow white owl represented the prayer and holiness prophets. These are watchers and prophetic intercessors. They are those who the Lord had sent to pray and intercede over cities and nations. From out of this prophetic bird has sprung the prayer and purity revival movements.

As I looked at these three birds that took flight, I noticed each one had a face of a man. The golden eagle look like a young prophet Bob Jones, his eyes piercing and laser-like, seeing directly into the heavens. The silver winged dove had the face of a young prophet Kenneth Hagin. His silver tipped wings released healing and deliverance to the nations. The snow white owl had the face of a young Leonard Ravenhill. His eyes pierced the darkest of night and carried the wisdom of the heavenly Father.

Birthing the White Swan

These three birds caught the fresh wind of the Spirit, and as they flew together, this new mantle was placed around their shoulders. When this happened, they changed into a white swan and began to fly with grace and splendor.

I heard the Lord say: "This is My Bridal company! Those who have an ear to hear what the Spirit is saying to the Church. If you will fly together as one, a new prophetic movement will come. A new bird will be released—one the enemy can't stop nor hinder, one that carries grace, glory and splendor. This bird will rise to new heights, she will win every war, battle, and fight. Nothing will be withheld from My heavenly hands, for I've called My Bride to stand. The hosts of Heaven will be at her command! So unite and see My power come, for I've called My Bride to overcome!"

This fourth, heavenly bird represents the heavenly Bride that carries the spirit of the overcomer.

This heavenly bird is one that God wants the Church to give birth to in the earth, in this hour. It's a heavenly bird of grace, glory, and power!

I believe we are in a season of acceleration in the prophetic. A new mantle is being offered to the Church. God is looking for leaders to unite from these three movements. As they come together in this season, a new, fresh wave of prophetic power will be released upon this young prophetic generation of sons and daughters. It will take the spirit of Elijah coming upon the fathers and mothers to unite the different prophetic movements, but they will release a Bridal company, and a new prophetic bird will be released in the earth, one the world has never seen before.

Charlie and Brynn Shamp, President and Founders

Appendix 2

Decrees that Shifted a Nation

Below is a list of some of the decrees released during STN 2017.

Decree: Ezekiel 36:26

> 'Australia, God gives you a new heart and puts a new spirit within you. He takes out your stoney heart and gives you a tender responsive heart'.
>
> 'Australia shift back to God! Shift your heart to loving the Lord your God. Shift into alignment with God's will and ways'.

Decree:

> 'God's throne will be established in our hearts. God's throne will be established in the nation!'

Decree:

> 'Australia, love the Lord your God with all your heart, soul, mind and strength.'

Decree:

> 'People of God, rise in the spirit and power of Elijah to turn and reconcile the heart of the nation to Father God!'

Decree:

> 'Rise in the 'forerunner anointing' of the spirit and power of Elijah. Prepare the way of the Lord!'

DAY 1: Matthew 22:37, Psalms 108:1, Psalms 119:111
Decree:

'Australia, love the Lord your God with all your heart, soul, mind and strength'.

'The Kingdom of God come and God's will be done in the nation'!

'Awaken Worshippers! Arise with fire on the altars of your hearts. Burn with the zeal of the Lord.'

'The altars' of our hearts will be places for His glory, fire and power to release heaven to earth.'

Decree to the hearts: 'Shift open to receive Jesus Christ to rule and reign as the Glory-King over you!'

We build altars of worship and establish His throne in the heart of Australia.

DAY 2: Luke 1:16-17
Decree:

'People of God, rise in the spirit and power of Elijah to turn and reconcile the heart of the nation to Father God!'

'Australia, turn to love God, as you did when you were first established as a nation on godly principles.'

'Prodigal nation, return to love God first and seek His Kingdom and His righteousness!'

'The Reformation has begun in the heart of Australia! Shift under God's Hand!'

'Hearts of fathers, turn to your children. Rebellious children accept and turn to fathers'.

'Families be reconciled all across this land, displaying the heart of the Father across this nation'.

APPENDIX   283

'Prodigals return home. Return to the Father's heart'.

DAY 3: Isaiah 35:8, 40:3
Decree:
'Rise in the 'forerunner anointing' of the spirit and power of Elijah. Prepare the way of the Lord'!
'Ancient paths open, ancient ways unlock for the coming King'!
'Sword of the Lord be released and cut through and prepare a 'highway of holiness' in the heart of the nation'.
'We release a spirit of worship and prayer. High Praises are rising, building the throne of the Glory-King over Australia'.
'Houses of Prayer, increase around the nation in the cities and towns and across the outback in hidden and indigenous communities'.
'We decree, the indigenous church will be 'heard' in the nation'.

DAY 4: Ephesians 1:16-20, Isaiah 11:2-3
Decree:
'The heart of Australia is flooded with light, to understand the confident hope God has given to his people, his nation'.
'The fullness of the Holy Spirit is pouring out, the spirit of wisdom and understanding, power and might and the knowledge of the fear of the Lord, convicting, convincing, shifting and turning hearts to Him with reverential awe and obedience'.
'We are led by the Spirit of the Lord and we move as He

moves'.

'Australia, turn back to worship Jesus Christ the King of Glory'!

We will see the manifestation of a 'heart shift' in the nation!

'This nation will understand the incredible greatness of God's power as she rises to believe'.

DAY 5: Isaiah 55:6, 2 Chronicles 7:14

Decree:

'Australia seeks the Lord while he may be found, calls upon Him because he is near'.

'The set time is now for every heart to find their first love and shift into a deeper knowledge of God'.

'The nation of Australia will be covered with the knowledge of the glory of the Lord'.

'The Father's love and goodness will shift hearts towards their redeemer'.

'A great move of God will come to cleanse, purify, deliver and heal the nation and shift us into a deeper place of peace and intimacy in the presence of the Lord'.

DAY 6: Proverbs 3:5

Decree:

'Australia, trust in the Lord with all your heart and learn not on your own understanding'.

'Worship Warriors Arise! Advance with one heart, one mind, one purpose, in one accord to shift the heart of this nation back to God'.

'Decree to the 'Heart of the Nation':- 'Shift', 'Align' to the Father's heart'.

'Align to God's will, God's ways, God's plans and purposes'.

'Fulfil your God given destiny as the great Southland of the Holy Spirit'.

'We decree the manifestation of a mighty 'Heart Shift' across the nation'.

DAY 7: Ezekiel 36:26, Zechariah 4:6, Isaiah 9:7

Decree:

'Australia, God gives you a new heart and puts a new spirit within you. He is takes out your stoney heart and gives you a tender responsive heart'.

'We release the passionate zeal of the Lord of Hosts to turn the heart of this nation to himself'.

'The wind of the Spirit is blowing to align the heart of the nation to God'.

'Australia, be established in your identity as the Great South Land of the Holy Spirit'.

'Heart of Australia, shift from unrighteousness to the righteousness of God'.

'Heart of this Nation - align into Covenant with God and His righteousness'.

'We open our hearts and the heart of this nation and declare, "Welcome to the King of Glory - Come in!"'

www.ingramcontent.com/pod-product-compliance
Lightning Source LLC
Chambersburg PA
CBHW070535010526
44118CB00012B/1140